Sex and Yoga:

A Journey of Self-Discovery

by Maggie Zurowska

Table of Contents

Title and Credits...4

Dedication...5

Introduction...6

Chapter 1: Doctor, Doctor...7

Chapter 2: New York Love Affair...12

Chapter 3: Backstory Break...24

Chapter 4: New Year, New Place...26

Chapter 5: Flashback, Flash Forward...31

Chapter 6: Up in the Air...37

Chapter 7: First Tango in Argentina...46

Chapter 8: New York State of Mind...63

Chapter 9: Canada, Oh, Canada...and Hamsa...72

Chapter 10: Mexico Lindo...81

Chapter 11: Back in the New York Groove.....85

Chapter 12: North to Alaska...99

Chapter 13: Mediation Vacation...105

Chapter 14: Big Changes in Little Brooklyn...116

Chapter 15: The Best Decision I Ever Made.....118

Chapter 16: Paradise.....121

Epilogue...136

Acknowledgements...138

About the Author...139

Sex and Yoga:
A Journey of Self-Discovery

By Maggie Zurowska

Cover layout by Justyna Faustyna Milczuk

Copyright © 2016
ISBN 978-0-692-84924-8

This book may not be reproduced or resold in whole or in part through print, electronic or any other medium.
All rights reserved.

Dedication

If you are reading this book, it means that the title caught your attention—either the sex or yoga aspect of it, or maybe both. Hopefully, my own experiences will give you something to think about.

I would like to dedicate this book to those who are learning how to stop, think, and analyze their actions so they can move forward with a new positive attitude. This is for those who are awakening and entering the spiritual path, despite what their past carried, who aren't afraid of change, no matter what future holds. I hope this book gives you the courage to move forward, to never stop learning about yourself, because after all, the key is you.

Introduction

At first, I wasn't sure if I had a book. But I did have a story. I believe that everyone has a story, and this is mine. I hope it will touch people. Teach people. I hope it will speak to you and others so that their own life path makes more sense to them by reading about mine and where it has led me. Into other people's arms, other people's beds, bad jobs, good jobs, terrible relationships and wonderful ones, to a quirky marriage, to disease. It propelled me into life-changing situations. And back home again.

Think of it as "The Travails of Maggie" or "The Perils of Promiscuousness."

This is my journey, through sex and yoga, and everything else in between. I'm glad you're along for the ride. Hold on tight!

MZ
2016

Chapter 1
Doctor, Doctor

There I was in New York City. It was December 24, 2012. Christmas Eve, my 33rd birthday. I was feeling like Jesus did at the same age: crucified.

And for what? For humanity? Or for all of those lovers I broke the sanctity of my marriage vows with and cheated on my husband with? Maybe it happened before I decided to get married. Maybe my husband "Apollo" was the reason I was lying down now with my legs spread wide, analyzing each and every one of my "forbidden fruit" moments of sexual ecstasy.

My attacker was a female Hindu gynecologist who was slowly killing me with her long spear. She stuck it in slowly but sharply, into the most sensitive part of me: my vagina. Why was she so brutal, I wondered? Was she punishing me for my copious sexual performances? Did she want me to feel guilty or maybe reprimand me for cursing the last time I was in her office?

"You Polish are usually so nice," she'd commented. "How come you're so rude, saying this bad word 'bitch' over and over again?"

Of course, I was rude! All politeness falls by the wayside when you hear the most killing news of your 33 "Jesus Years:"

> "You have the HPV virus. You need to have surgery to get rid of it because it can lead to cancer."

All I heard was virus and cancer. I didn't know what HPV meant, but it didn't sound good.

On the way home from the doctor's office, I tried to process the message. Feeling guilty, I tried to accept my karma—maybe I deserved this diagnosis. Maybe I deserved it for being a slut, a whore.

Christmas Eve was a peaceful time for the rest of the world, but not for me. Not that year. Lonely and alone, I mourned for my best friend: my pussy. Could it be cured? Was it all worth it? What would happen to my New Year's resolution for 2013? To become a sex expert and perfect lover. I guess I'd have to find another resolution. Being free with my body could kill me.

My head was spinning. I could hear the voice of my ex-girlfriend, Arron. Her words when we parted were trapped inside my head and wouldn't be silenced. I could see her and hear her everywhere, taunting me with, 'Maggie when I leave, you'll be back sleeping with everyone under the sun again.'

Oh, sweet Arron, you're the only one who knows the truth about me. Maybe I am a slut, but still, I'm a good person trying to reach her Buddha-hood so badly. And maybe in a bad way—on her back, on her knees, with all sorts of lovers, male, female and everything else in between.

But still, I'm not an evil person. I have good career, my own apartment in Brooklyn, a car and friends. I follow my dreams, and try to be decent and honest with others. I think I'm attractive on the outside and beautiful on the inside, always hungry for knowledge. I read a lot, travel as much as I can, do sports, yoga, and recently, even have tried to meditate with Beatrice, "my new, slutty friend," as Arron likes to call her. (To clarify, "my new slutty friend" has the same energy I do, is beautiful and yes, we've already exchanged some tasty kisses.)

In my quest for self-improvement, I even got married and made a strong attempt to be heterosexual. Was it a wrong move? Is my husband the one who infected me with HPV? Or was it one of the many women I was with since my oh-so-reasonable ex girlfriend broke up with me two years ago?

After seven years of being together, I noticed that even though we're not a couple any longer, Arron still plays a huge role in my life. People always say that you should forget your ex and move on. The "moving on" part I achieved, but I still struggle with the first one. I can't forget Arron. She exists in my life not only emotionally, but also physically—or, as some might say, psycho-physically, the double PP theory.

Oddly enough, Arron was the legal witness at my wedding ceremony. When I decided to get married to my wonderful husband Apollo, she was there to sign my marriage license and to support us during that significant moment. That's not the only paradox in our relationship—there are several. Arron's parents have stayed at my place when they visited from Poland because her place (which she shares with her new girlfriend!), located in the Windsor Terrace section of Brooklyn, overlooking Prospect Park with a breathtaking view, was too small. But mine, a few blocks away on Ocean Avenue, was just right.

Arron's folks even came to my wedding ceremony. We were like a one big, happy, dysfunctional, Millennial New York family: my husband Apollo, my ex and her parents. We all left my apartment together and went to Brooklyn's City Hall, where I would begin my new life. I was excited even though I felt like an actor playing a role in a sitcom. But I gave my high-heels a practice walk and decided to go for it. I figured, if I could learn how to walk on such uncomfortable feminine things, I would also able to accept my new marriage status and give heterosexuality shot. At the time, nothing could stop me, although now I realize what a big mistake it was. What's that saying about hindsight being 20/20?

At my wedding dinner with my complex group of family and friends, news broke that New York State had just legalized gay marriage. Staring at the restaurant's TV screen with my mouth open wide, I couldn't believe what I'd just heard. I took a deep sip of Merlot, smiled at my ex, softly squeezed my husband's leg under the table and gently nudged Jasmine, the beautiful Asian friend I was currently hot for. Both Apollo and Jasmine responded at the same time—with big smiles. Was my marriage to Apollo doomed or was the gay marriage ruling a good omen? I didn't want to think about it. I was just happy with what everyone, including the whole world and me, had just accomplished. To celebrate, I ordered Jack and Coke, and cheered on what the future would bring. The show must go on, right? I laugh couldn't help but laugh.

And I'm still laughing. But this time it's a different type of laugh. It's more dramatic, full of tears and pain. My first 32 years on the planet were almost over and there I was, celebrating my 33rd birthday with my Indian gynecologist, who I've barely even seen since she began crouching between my legs with her not-so-magic wand. Her professional poker face was practically in my pussy, leaving no chance for eye contact or even small-talk to soften the blow of what she just told me. I was aching for at least one smile or even meaningless babble about the weather just to cheer me up the tragic moment she delivered my HPV diagnosis. I realize now it was too much to ask for. After all, she was just a doctor, not a savior.

Disappointed, I tried to find my savior somewhere else. I turned to Buddha. When I got home from the doctor's office, I chanted for hours. I was seeking peace of mind but ended up with a huge headache instead. Every whisper, every single word, every orgasm from my past is what I received in return. My memories—past loves, past words, past caresses, past climaxes—all began to expand inside my head. They started taking on extremely large shapes, getting bigger and more unruly by the second. Soon, I couldn't even control them anymore. I they hung like a heavy cloud over my head. I put on the ceiling fan to try to chase the memory cloud away, but of course, it didn't help. Damn my sins! Damn me, I thought.

WARNING:

Girls! (And guys!) HPV is a serious problem in the United States, especially in New York City. The statistics show that about 80% of sexually-active adults will have been infected with the HPV virus before the age of 50. This makes it the most common sexually-transmitted virus. It should be treated seriously because if not taken care of, it could lead to cervical cancer for women. Men can pass along the HPV "cancer" virus to their partners. Most people who have HPV don't even know they have it. This is because they don't develop genital warts or other outward signs of HPV.

Even though the HPV virus is most often transmitted via vaginal or anal intercourse, it can also be contracted through genital-to-genital contact and through oral sex. Condoms are protective, but not 100% because they don't shield the entire genital region. So, please be safe, get tested for HPV. And get the vaccine!

One of the reasons I've written this book is to educate others about the dangers of HPV, and so they can learn from my mistakes...and triumphs.

Read on!

Chapter 2
New York Love Affair

For the entire seven years, I was with Arron, I never cheated on her.

Well, I did kiss someone, but don't consider kissing cheating. I kissed the other girl without even knowing her name. Kissing is such a normal thing for me, almost like breathing. Sometimes I kiss, then realize mid-kiss that don't know who I'm kissing. Maybe this is because I'm so bad at remembering names. Or maybe it's because a name is not as important as a kiss. The very act of kissing, and the rest that follows, including names, pales in comparison to a first kiss.

I'm pretty sure that I'm not the only one who struggles with names. Especially American names. I was born Malgorzata. But I left Malgorzata in Poland. In the US, I am Maggie, an entirely different person. But I digress...

Names. New York is full of strange names from all over the world. Often, the same name is used for people of both genders. Confusing, because this sometimes causes misunderstandings and awkward situations.

Once, I was dancing with a guy and then with a girl downtown at the famous gay bar in Greenwich Village known as Stonewall. (The gay rights movement pretty much began there during the Stonewall Riots of 1969. But I digress again.) The next day, I woke up to a text from Toni, who tried to invite me for a date. I thanked her for a great, fun night but politely rejected her advances, tagging on that she was beautiful, to soften the blow. In response, I received this nasty text:

"Fuck you, stupid les. I'm not a girl that you wish me to be"

What happened? The texter on the other end was a he, not a she. What the hell was a straight guy doing in the gay bar? Trying to pick up gay women? It wasn't the best place to pick up a straight girl. Well, I tried to be nice and should get some Brownie points for recognizing the name, even though it was a case of mistaken identity.

Back to my ex, Arron. As I said, I never cheated on her. I tried to be extremely honest in our long relationship. I had a great time, a magical seven years. We were lovers, friends and we fulfilled each other in all ways. As happy as we were together, I was sure we'd be partners forever. I was convinced Arron was "the one." My girl. My soulmate. The love of my life. But it wasn't to be. I was to learn that "forever" wasn't a very long time. At least for Arron and me.

Our very deep relation based on balance—Arron gave me what I was missing and I did the same for her. We filled in the missing jigsaw puzzle pieces in each other. Arron was very orderly and organized while I had a crazy, spontaneous personality. She was the responsible one with her both feet firmly on the ground while I was the innocent, crazy, free spirit, bouncing through the sky like a helium balloon on the breeze. Arron kept me tethered; I set her free. We fulfilled each other. For a time. But nothing lasts, at least not for me. Arron and I grew in different directions. When we realized this, that our relationship no longer worked, we decided to split peacefully, before we destroyed the things in each other that we'd once loved.

But I'll never forget the day Arron and I met. It was through a friend of hers. It was in Rye, New York, a small upstate town that's very popular with lesbians, for some reason. At the beginning of my stay in the US I worked and lived with a host family as an au pair. (A fancy French term that basically means "babysitter.") Arron was an au pair, too. Angel, gorgeous, famous town lesbian, noticed me at Starbucks, the only place that offered any kind of recreation in that sleepy, suburban town. Rye's Starbucks was known as the best place to pick up someone and a neighborhood hot spot for teens to meet—and date.

My European very short, very spiky haircut caught Angel's eye, who figured I must be gay with hair as short as that. (In Europe, nobody would categorize me as gay just because of a haircut. They're much more evolved!) Back then, I even wasn't even sure I was gay myself. Today, I consider myself a bisexual, though some would doubt even that, arguing that true bisexuality doesn't exist. Either you're gay or not. Period. End of story.

I love to argue this "gay-or-not" premise in a hot debate, defending my theory. Yes, for bisexual girls it is possible to have great multiple orgasms with a man and a woman. And yes, we are able to fall in love with both sexes. I don't like to put labels on feelings and emotions or neatly place a frame around them as you might do to a photograph. To me, each case is different. I don't like close-minded people who, in search of logic, categorize others as either as straight or gay. I believe it's not so much about gender but about the person we fall in love with. You can't deny that there are more people like me who enjoy intimacy with both sexes and appreciate the beautiful bodies and souls of both men and women. It's the best of both worlds.

To me, guys are like a dominant Apollo—you know, the Greek god—glistening with sweaty muscles, with power dripping from all of their body parts, especially their erect penis. (This is why I nicknamed my dear husband "Apollo" in this book.) And on the opposite side of the equation, there is a tempting, tantalizing Eve with her forbidden and tasty "apple," and lovely, delicate curves. Man is simplicity, while woman is complexity. With a man, it's all out there in the open, but with a woman, it's hidden, like a ripe fruit that must be discovered, uncovered, and appreciated. This is how I see both sexes.

Isn't it in our nature that we are all seeking balance? So, why not have both, male and female, when seeking this balance?

And this is exactly is what I was looking for moment Angel discovered me at Starbuck's. Balance. Some magical other person to help balance me out. Angel happily announced, "This is Maggie, the new les in town!" to everyone in Starbucks who cared to listen. Perhaps knowing that there would be a spark between us, Angel gave me the telephone number of her friend Arron, who was a Polish nanny, just like me. Angel thought Arron and I would hit it off. (She was right!) I called Arron soon after I got home.

She and I made plans to meet a few days later at the MetroNorth train station. As I drove there, I was eating a huge apple. That large, red fruit almost obstructed my view of the road through the windshield. I couldn't really see what was on the other side of the wheel. I just envisioned it, guessed it, pictured it. New in town, new to New York roads, new to genetically-engineered American "healthy fruit," when I saw Arron, for the first time, I almost choked on my apple.

Arron suggested I follow her to Starbucks and shifted her car into gear. As if choking wasn't enough, by mistake, I drove the wrong way down a one-way street. By sheer luck, no one was coming in my direction. I was suddenly disorientated by seeing this beautiful woman waiting for me at the train station. Luckily, I didn't cause an accident. But at that point I didn't really care, because for the first time in my life, I had a deep, intense feeling for another human being just by looking at her. I somehow knew that Arron was "the one." I wanted her to be mine, now and forever. To hell with everything else.

When I first laid eyes on Arron, I was immediately taken with her. She was strong, powerful, thickly built, with long, brown hair. Arron looked like a tough girl, with a pretty but serious face. And her eyes...they were somewhere between blue and green, more of a gray. They could be sarcastic and judgmental one minute and soft as a kitten's the next. Arron's gaze was brutally honest. When she looked at me, I felt strangely violated, like she was undressing me in a glance. But I liked it!

When Arron walked, it was as though the whole earth shook in response to the positive vibes she gave out. Even though we haven't been together for several years, thoughts of her still shake me to the core.

To this day, I can't explain the strange feeling I had when I met Arron. Maybe we had known each other in a past life. All I can say is that it was love at first sight. Arron looked like someone I knew I could trust, someone who could take care of herself—and me! —at the same time. This is exactly what I needed at the time. I felt so frightened and vulnerable being in a strange country, all alone. I didn't know what the future held for me. But I did know that somehow, my future involved this lovely, rough girl named Arron.

From the start, Arron was always very caring and a great giver. She had a huge heart, and gave everything more than 100%. She cared last about herself and always put the person she was with first. (Still does.) But as thoughtful as she was, Arron was also a perfectionist. Nothing could be done better than the way she did it. Plus her ideas were always the best ideas. Ever. Yours were always second-rate, no matter how good they were. That's how my Arron was. At first, I accepted it but after a while, it became tiresome.

Many years have passed since Arron and I have been together but I still remember how good it felt to be "the one" for her. The one Arron chose to be with. I knew we were going to stay together no matter what.

With butterflies in my stomach, my first date with Arron turned to be my best ever. After Starbucks, we went to Applebee's and laughed the whole four hours we were there, barely tasting the terrible cookie-cutter, chain restaurant food, chatting happily in Polish, a language I missed speaking.

I remember a man sitting at the bar next to us. He was tall, a bit tipsy. It seemed like he was having a hard time dealing with the cards he was dealt. The man downed shots of straight-up whiskey way too fast. It was as if he was trying to drown out the bad things from his life. From the corner of his eye, the man watched Arron and me. He sent us a drunken smile and moved even closer, treating us to the scent of fermenting alcohol on his breath. "Hey girls," he said, "You must know each other a long time."

"Why do you think so?" I asked him.

He replied, "Well, I don't understand a word of what you're saying, but I can tell from your body language that you feel real comfortable with each other." Then he tagged on, just to be funny, "Or is it the Margarita you're drinking?"

"It's not the Margarita," Arron said. "And we just met." Her eyes were hard, unfriendly, silently suggesting that he should leave us alone.

But the drunken man wouldn't be swayed. "Nah, I don't believe you," he drawled and turned back to his almost-empty glass.

Drunk as he was, the man's disbelief struck me to the core. Even though Arron and I had just met, it was as if our souls had known each other many years before. I felt this with Arron many times afterwards, often when I was cradled in her arms. I felt complete, like I'd found my second half, when I lay there with her.

I was so grateful Arron was in my life. She was everything to me. She had it all—everything I couldn't find in a man. Arron was brave, strong, and there was nothing she couldn't do or take care of. Everything she did was well planned and organized. Every trip we ever took had been scratched out on paper first, and worked out to the last detail: places to visit, motels, and food stops, day by day. Basically, Arron kept control of everything and she did it very well. I felt secure with her. I didn't need to worry about anything. I was in a comfortable "love zone" and forgot about all the worries in my previous, uncontrolled life.

But as the years passed, Arron's "take charge" attitude had become a huge issue. With Arron calling all the shots in our lives, I didn't have to think for myself. I didn't have to make decisions. At first, it was wonderful but then it became tiresome. I lost sight of myself—who Maggie was, what Maggie wanted, what Maggie thought. But in the beginning of our relationship, I loved being Arron's princess. I was amazed at how I, who was usually such a cocky little flirt, was absolutely dedicated to her. I was suddenly very serious about relationships, about life. It was all new to me and had never really happened to me before.

I accepted this new stage in my life for seven years, turning down other options and possible dates. And it was all because I had been chosen by the best. My Arron.

Arron had waltzed into my life at the ideal time, right around an epic failed date with a Peruvian guy named Dick. So I was ripe and ready for the woman who would become my soul mate. I'd met Dick in a Westchester bar. Although I was already dating Arron, we weren't "exclusive" yet. The horrible date with Dick (which turned out to be a perfect name for this idiot!) was about to change my feelings about committed relationships for good.

Dick called me the day after he and I met, saying, "Hey, Maggie I know this great place. You'd love it but I won't tell you where it is. Please, let's go out together so I can take you there."

I was intrigued. It sounded like the makings for an exciting date. Enthusiastically, I replied, "Sure, I love surprises. I'll see you Saturday."

I hung up the phone, thrilled about the prospect of my first New York date with a guy. I checked the mirror, searching for my best look, critically examining my spiked hair. For a quick moment, I wished it was longer and that I looked more fem. But in the next breath, I decided that I liked the way I looked and I figured Dick did too or else he wouldn't have called me. Little did I know that I shouldn't have worried about how I looked at all. Not for this bozo.

I was supposed to meet Dick in Manhattan, another exciting prospect for me. Suburban au pairs don't get out of town much. And we don't ride on commuter trains much, especially on weekends. So I didn't realize that Metro-North train schedules are different on Saturdays. Not only do the train times change but some don't even run at all. Maybe seasoned commuters know this but not Polish girls new to the 'burbs like me.

I left home with the best intentions, full of hope, expecting to have the greatest date ever in this legendary Sex and the City place. Just like Miranda and Carrie did on the TV show. Commuting from Westchester to New York City usually took about an hour but my journey was an ordeal from the start. Missed trains, trains that never came...I was a mess before I even arrived at Grand Central Station. I tried as best I could to fix myself up in the restroom mirror, which was quite a feat on a speeding train.

When we finally pulled into Grand Central, I barely noticed its impressive Beaux Arts architecture and sweeping curved ceiling decorated with stars and constellations. My head was swirling with the exciting promise of my date with Dick and the city itself. I didn't think about anything else.

Eager, I brushed away any self-doubt I had about being new to the States. I still wasn't comfortable with speaking English, though I was getting better every day. I ducked into a bathroom once more to check the damage the train ride from Hell had done. I made a few adjustments of my hair and makeup in the smeared mirror, sent myself a smile to bolster my ego. With confidence, I strutted out of the grungy train station bathroom.

Full of hope, I definitely didn't plan on spending my whole day underground. But that's how I spent most of it: riding trains. Dick's idea of a "great place" for our date happened to be the Bronx Zoo. I was so disappointed. I dreamed of exploring the city on the arm of a handsome man but instead, he was carting me off to a smelly zoo in the outer boroughs.

'No way!' I said to myself when Dick excitedly revealed his plans. I didn't want to be in a zoo on a Saturday with hundreds of screaming kids and their paranoid parents chasing after them. Besides, I'm allergic to half the animals there. He has to be joking, I thought. Or else, he was a jerk, which is what he turned out to be. This was not only my first date, but my first time in New York City itself. I was dying for being a part of the vivid scene that appeared before me outside the doors of Grand Central Station. But instead, I was going to the zoo.

Even worse, is that the Bronx Zoo is a long subway ride from midtown Manhattan. The "5" train that goes there was out of service that day. No other option was available. Reluctantly, Dick said we could take a cab, which I knew would cost a fortune. I'd rather he spend it on a nice brunch in an outdoor café somewhere in Midtown. I didn't want to go to the freaking zoo! What was I, five-years-old? No, I was a young, single woman itching to spend the day in the most exciting city in the world with a hot guy. Instead, I was going to look at elephants.

But that didn't end up happening either. Instead, I shared my day with Dick and the MTA, their staff and customers. We never left the underground besides wandering around Grand Central Terminal. We ran for trains the whole time we spent together. For three hours we rode around in circles, and didn't even get to the Bronx Zoo. My date with Dick was one big disappointment after another.

Angry, disappointed and stressed out, I took the train back home to Westchester. I tried to calm myself down by daydreaming about my new friend Arron. Would I have the nerve to take her on as a lover? Would Arron want me? I already felt so close to her, even after one date. I didn't think I could ever have the same rapport with someone like Dick, who had really lived up to his name that afternoon.

It was almost as though my thoughts of Arron magically summoned her because she unexpectedly showed up on the Metro-North train that was heading back to Westchester. As if out of a dream, Arron just appeared in the train car. Was she there because I willed it to happen? Or was it just a happy coincidence.

It turned out that Arron had spent her day in the city as well. (But her day was a lot better than mine!) I couldn't believe that in this city of eight million people, she just happened to pop up on my train. Manhattan Island is small geographically, just 22 miles from south to north, but stuffed with so many people. It's amazing that you always seem to meet someone you know, especially on a train heading in the same direction.

But this wasn't a total coincidence. True, Arron was meeting a friend in the City but she also knew that I was going a date. She hoped she would run into me on my way back. "Right on time," Arron said smiling, taking the seat next to me.

"What are you doing here?" I wondered. "Following me?"

Arron laughed. "Well, since I met you, yes."

I didn't know on what to say. Arron was so straightforward and confident in her response that I was speechless. She had already told me that when she sees something she wants, she goes for it right away. Little did I know that she was talking about me. She always cut to the chase—and I was the chase. Arron had no time for meaningless words or flirting, which I enjoyed immensely. To her, flirting was a meaningless, time-wasting game. I decided to play hers.

Still shocked by her brazen response, I decided to be just as brazen as Arron was. I convinced myself, 'Okay, let's give this a try.' I took a deep breath and asked Arron if she had any plans. "Do you want to go for a drink?" I wondered. "My date sucked. I can really use one."

I was thrilled when she agreed. "I know a good place near the station."

So, my rendezvous with a guy ended up being with a girl but I was game for anything. Arron won the battle for my affection with determination and confidence. Besides that, she turned me on. Little did I know that night, I would give up on men for next few years because my heart was stolen by a woman.

After a few shots of tequila, Arron laid down the law. "Who do you want? Me or him? Because I don't play games and I won't wait for you any longer." I almost dropped my shot glass on the floor. Arron was so self-assured. Without any hesitation, I chose her and I would do it over and over again.

From the start, it was wonderful with Arron. We were together day and night. I forgot about men and let myself be carried away by my lesbian lover. Like a child being led by the hand through the fog, I trusted where Arron would take me. Everything was new and exciting. I felt like a Slavic Alice in a Westchester Wonderland because everything around me was so animated and dreamlike. I was new to New York as well as to the gay world. I discovered them both simultaneously and reveled in them equally.

At times, I felt like I was too much for Arron, though. My imagination and creativity almost put us into a few embarrassing situations. Once, I decided that we should visit a "hot sheets" motel. That's a seedy hotel where you go just for sex and they rent rooms by the hour. Arron wasn't as into it as I was. I admit, I did have my doubts when we arrived at the shabby-looking motel. Even moreso when we got to the room, where you could hear the sex through the walls. Part of me found it stimulating, being in a place where people went only to fuck. I felt like an actress in a porn movie. (I'm adventurist...I can't help it!) My sexuality was in full bloom that evening. I had a very straight upbringing, so I loved feeling like a dirty girl. Arron didn't enjoy playing the part of slut as much as I did, but went along with it for my sake.

In our threadbare room, Arron pointed to the bed in disgust. "Maggie, it's so nasty in here! Look at that long, dark hair on the pillow."

I tried to brighten up a bad situation. "Just pick it off and pretend it was never there." I was so aroused being in this seedy place with my new lover that I was prepared to ignore almost anything. "Let's do it on the floor," I offered.

Arron thought this was an even worse idea. "Are you crazy? It probably hasn't been vacuumed in years." She studied the filthy carpet as though she were looking for bloodstains. "I'm sorry darling," Arron finally said, "But I just can't. Let's go back home, I really prefer my own bed."

Disappointed, I agreed. "But I just want you to know that I don't really care how this place looks. I could make love to you anywhere."

But Arron was unmoved. "So, do you want me or is the only thing you care about having sex in this filthy place?"

I thought for a minute. "The idea itself," I told her.

"Are you serious? Does it really turn you on?" Arron wondered.

She had me trapped yet again. "I love you," I said, just as Arron wanted to hear. "Let's go back home." But I didn't really mean it. I gave her a kiss and apologized for my odd (and dirty) desires.

There were a few more instances where my vivid imagination put Arron and me into awkward situations. Another time, it was the dead of winter, and we were in the middle of a mountain, skiing, when I suddenly desired her, right then and there. Maybe it had something to do with watching Arron, a brand new skier, taking on the Black Diamonds fearlessly, but I was hopelessly turned on. We made our way down the hill and headed straight to the ski lodge's bathroom. In a rush, we forgot to take off our ski boots. Wiggling out of padded pants with our boots still on was a challenge but I was up for it. Somehow, Arron and I managed to pleasure each other, but it took a long time for us to finish. When we were done, I couldn't feel my legs. Whether it was from trying to balance in the heavy boots or from climaxing, I'll never know.

Adventure has always been a huge aphrodisiac for me. I was eager to experience new, different and wild sex with my new love, especially in the outdoors. One afternoon on a hike in the woods with Arron, I felt super connected with nature—and horny. I was ready make love with her in the middle of the forest. Once again, my desire took over and I stopped being practical. I conveniently forgot about one thing: bugs. While Arron and I romped in the high grass, ticks and other insects began feasting on my blood. Eventually, I got "there" but I had dozens of bug bites all over my body as a souvenir.

But even this wasn't enough to teach me to be less wild and more cautious. Another day, Arron and I went to a gay bar in a nearby Westchester town. After few drinks, tipsy and horny, we began making out in our car in the parking lot. I was on top of Arron, with my breasts covering her face, moving back and forth. The whole car moved with us, bouncing up and down, pumping in the same rhythm. The car windows got steamy, and soon, the whole club came outside to watch us—Arron's friends, too. We didn't realize it until after we were done. Arron was horrified…but satisfied. I was too.

Over the seven years Arron and I were a couple, I put us through a few more embarrassing and awkward situations. But overall, our time together was stable and lovely. We fulfilled each other, especially in the beginning. But as with many relationships, after a time, Arron and I discovered that our paths started drifting in different directions. She wanted a family; I wanted fun. I wasn't ready to settle down and have children, even with Arron. To her, life was a serious matter, while to me, every day was a chance for a new adventure. Although we shared many memories, and had a beautiful past together, that's just it...the best of our relationship was in the past. Both of us knew it. The love just wasn't there anymore. We both accepted the fact that it was time to move on.

Sadly, Arron and I separated, each trying to rebuild our lives, struggling to shift from a partnership to a friendship. Arron and I tried to preserve our relationship and the closeness we'd achieved. But even being "just friends" was difficult at first—maybe because we'd been so much more to each other.

I moved on, tried not to look back. I struggled to look ahead toward the future and whatever it might hold for me. New York was still a new, exciting city, and I felt like I'd barely scratched its surface. I was ready to open the door, come out to play, and explore more.

Chapter 3
Backstory Break

At this point in the adventure, I thought you might be curious about where it all started and how I went from there to here...and where exactly "there" was.

I was born and raised in Zakopane, a small but well-known city in the mountains of south Poland. From the very start, my life was full of fun, excitement and adrenaline. I loved exploring the hills, climbing trees and playing outdoors. As a kid, I was surrounded by people who loved extremes too. We enjoyed high-risk sports like rock climbing, skiing, scuba-diving, sky diving, hiking and exploring caves. Some of my friends actually died doing these sports or by helping others when they worked as part of the rescue patrol in the mountains. That was my reality.

My family was very liberal and open-minded. They were always involved in the political changes that shaped Poland. My friends and I were as well. Talk of politics dominated my home. My dad, who was my hero, was well known in our town as a president of the solidarity movement. Then he became Deputy for Congress and Vice Minister of Culture. My mom was President of the town's Liberty Party.

My parents' political involvement influenced me and my sister Joana, who was two years older than me. Joana and I participated in each election by distributing flyers, collecting votes and doing anything we could to support the cause. It was great to be involved but it was also difficult. Why? Because I had the feeling that people looked at me through my parents' achievements, not my own. That's one of the reasons I felt I had to leave Poland. Achievements, self-realization and education was of primo importance in my home, and I wanted to be recognized by my own accomplishments.

My mom and dad gave Joana and me a lot of freedom. Their goal was to teach us how to be independent and follow our dreams. They had an "open marriage," so I think this had a big impact on me too. At home, I didn't have an example of a stabile monogamous relationship. An open relationship was the norm to me. So was being bisexual.

When I was a little older, my family has spent a lot of time in a village called Niedzica, where my dad was Director of Niedzica Castle. It was a beautiful, dramatic old building, perched on a cliff overlooking Czorsztyn Lake. I loved playing hide-and-seek in with my friends in the old castle. Later on, when my dad was Vice Minister of Culture, I enjoyed participating in cultural events, flirting and playing around at concerts, castles and palaces in the area. It was a great life.

Since my uncle was the Polish ambassador to Israel, my family traveled there often. I grew to love that country and its conflicts became the subject of my studies and my future profession. I specialized in Middle East conflict and Jewish-Polish relations. I was involved in the peace process and in rebuilding the bond between those two countries. My visits to Israel were frequent. I even worked on a kibbutz.

Once, when my sister and I were on a plane to Israel, there was a bomb scare. We were all terrified, even though it was a false alarm. But my poor parents, who were home in Poland, freaked out. Especially after there was an explosion in a Tel Aviv disco soon around the same time. The Intifada was in full swing. (The word "Intifada" literally means "tremor" in Arabic and is used to describe the Palestinian uprising against Israel in the West Bank of Gaza.) While the First Intifada was in 1987, here we were in the 1990s and the tremors of terror were still happening.

I promised my mother to put aside my plans to move to Israel to work and study there. Instead I came to the United States to brush up on my English. That's how I ended up in that au pair program where I met Arron. And the rest, as they say, is history.

Chapter 4
New Year, New Place

    After Arron and I split up, I felt lost, adrift, untethered. But I was determined not to wallow in sadness. I made a promise to myself that I would go out into the world and try new things. One of the new things I tried was being a tour guide. I was hired by a tour company to take Polish-speaking people on long-distance bus tours. One of stops: Florida, the Sunshine State.

    As enjoyable and glamorous as this might sound, it isn't. Working as a tour guide requires a huge amount of patience and heavy-duty psychology skills. Right after I boarded my people on the bus, I did a quick scan and tried to guess who they were (careers, personalities, etc.) and what I could expect from them. You know, who was a complainer, who was a jerk, who was cool, who was a horndog. My sexual sense button was always on. Either I received erotic vibes from someone or I didn't. My first time as a tour guide, no one struck my sexual fancy, which was probably just as well. My life was complicated enough as it was. I gave my driver the signal to start the bus's engine and take me away from New York—and my complex life.

    New Year's Eve, I decided to spend quietly, by myself. The events of the 2012 had put me into contemplative state of mind...for now. I wasn't looking forward to greeting 2013. I'd caught a cold and was feeling sick, even in Florida's warm weather. At 8 pm, I was already in a deep sleep at the Sunrise Motel in Fort Lauderdale. It was a perfect name for the place because watching the sun come up from its deck was gorgeous. A bit upset that I'd missed the fireworks and New Year Eve's beach party the night before, I was treated to a beautiful sunrise the next morning.

    I realized that my body, mind and soul needed a few quiet days to refuel. I'd had too much fun the year before and it had taken its toll on me. After Arron, I partied a little too much, dated more than one person at a time, and drank to excess. My tour groups in 2012 were full of odd people who partied even harder than I did. I finally had nice, quiet group of twenty Poles to take around for ten days. They weren't too demanding and I had more time for myself on this trip.

I found peace of mind in Florida. Part of it had to do with staying away from my people as much as I could. Not the best tactic for a tour guide, I admit, but it worked. I hid out when I had a free moment. I was trying to turn over a new leaf and was giving my all to meditation. This is something one of my best friends, Ms. Om, introduced me to a short time ago. "Maggie, you should try meditation to calm your mind and find balance in your life," she suggested.

"You're absolutely right," I agreed. "But I don't think balance wants to find me." We both laughed but I still gave Ms. Om my pinky promise to at least try mediation. Clearing my mind of all thoughts was a big challenge. There always seemed to be something bouncing around my head. With some obstacles, I was able to make progress in meditation. Eventually.

In search for my Mecca, my peaceful place, I discovered that the best place for me to meditate was the bathroom. Nobody bothers you there. It's an almost spiritual temple, a private space. Although sometimes I forgot to inform the others I was taking a much-needed breather, and I ended up in the company of 20 people. (My tour groups followed me everywhere I went, like sheep.) When this happened one time too many, I had to find another temple. Behind the motel in Orlando there was a nice deck by a lake. We always stayed at this motel a couple of days before heading to Miami and nobody else seemed to know about the beautiful deck. It became my perfect place for meditation and morning yoga. But Florida mornings can get pretty cold, so I often caught a chill while chilling on the deck. My windy morning yoga spot was the reason I spent my New Year's Eve in bed in Fort Lauderdale—I'd caught a cold on the breezy deck.

A year before, in 2012, I spent a wild New Year's Eve with another tour group. I'd been so drunk that I lost my sandals while giving them a dance demonstration on the hotel dance floor. Looking back, this was the beginning of the end during my crazy "Christ Year." As time went on, I started to feel like Jesus—crucified.

At the New Year's Eve bash that began 2012, I was hitting on one lady from my group the entire time. I'd noticed her from Day One, when she boarded the bus in New York City. Mary was smart, funny and classy, totally my type. I liked her sense of humor and felt we connected right away. I was intrigued and wanted to know her better. I sensed we would get closer as the tour went on. Mary wasn't just an anonymous number on my tour, she was much more. The vibes were definitely there but they weren't sexual. Yet. Although Mary looked like she could be my mother's age, I was still drawn to her. And I was always up for a challenge, in and out of bed. I just had to be patient.

It would be another few months before Mary and I kissed—which eventually happened, but back in New York. So, in Florida, besides waiting for that first kiss, I decided to take some action. But first, I had to inform Mary, my prospective Sugar Mama, that I appreciated girls as well as guys. She seemed surprised but also curious. As usual, there were tons of questions:

"How long have you been bisexual?"
"How is it?"
And finally, "How does it really work?" (I.e. how you do this lesbian thing?)

When Mary and I met for wine and a bite to eat, she immediately asked, "So, Maggie, were you always a lesbian?"

"I guess," I told her.

Mary laughed but I could tell she still wasn't satisfied with my answer. "But have you ever slept with a guy?"

"I'm married," was my response.

With confusion clouding her face, Mary gently asked, "So, how come? Are you bi, then?"

"Nah," I admitted. "I believe in bisexuality but I appreciate girls more."

Mary didn't believe what I said and neither did I. She just told me, "Maggie, you're crazy."

What else could I say? "I know," I told her. "I just have sex with my hubby from time to time. But like pussies more."

Instead of satisfying Mary's curiosity, there were more questions:

"When was your first time?"
"How was it?"

"Are you the guy or the girl when you do it?"
And the best one, "How the fuck you do it?"

    Already tired of getting grilled about my sexuality, I bit my lip and patiently tried to answer Mary's questions one by one, giving her the best answers I could. Right away, I understood that if something were to happen with Mary, it would be a game, nothing more. She was clearly straight, just bi-curious. Meaning she was ready to try bisexuality just to see how it worked. She didn't have anything to lose. Even though I knew that all I'd amount to would be a little experiment for her, I let the flirting game continue. I did enjoy it, though, up to a point. It was light, funny, a new experience. Mary and I became good friends, in spite of my reservations. Our friendship blossomed in Florida and continued up to New York.

    Mary and I kissed for the first time on a beautiful April night. It was at a barbecue at a friend's house. A pleasant evening, full of good food, good drink and good people, Mary and I were having a nice, long talk, when all of a sudden, she jumped back onto the gay/lesbian truck. While I liked Mary a lot, I was getting tired of hearing the same, old questions which I tried to answer the same, old way. Exasperated, I finally said, "Enough! Just try me!" and we kissed. It was as simple as that.

    I have to admit it was a long, nice kiss. There was even an audience, so I almost expected applause. Mary's daughter (who was two years younger than me) was sitting right next to us. She didn't say anything, just smiled and walked out. 'Well done, Maggie!' I told myself. 'You got yourself in trouble again!' But I couldn't resist kissing Mary. It had been a long time coming. And besides, it was my Sugar Mama who finally said that I could call her by her "new name"—Sugar Mama. I was glad she approved of my pet name for her.

    Our first kiss wasn't earth-shattering. It wasn't super-romantic. It was just a sweet, naive kiss with the promise of more to come. Nothing more happened that night but I knew it probably would soon. Even though I was sure Mary's interest in bisexuality—and me—wasn't serious, I still wondered how far it would take us. In the end, it was further than we expected—we wound up in bed with two guys who happened to be our friends. And even worse, it was during a trip with my ex, Arron and her wife Elaine. It seems I was always getting myself into hot water.

In an attempt to show Arron that we could still have a platonic relationship, I invited Arron and Elaine to join me and a few friends on a trip to New England. I really liked Elaine and thought she was a perfect match for my ex. Elaine was down to earth but with a dash of intuition and spirituality. Full of believe in friendship after relationship, I put a lot of energy into trying to make this "friendship" concept real, hoping it would work. But the truth was that I had a hard time being "just friends" with Arron after we were no longer lovers. In fact, I failed miserably at it.

The trip itself was enjoyable. We had a great time hiking all day and partying all night. One evening, a bunch of us met in one of our motel rooms. I've found that the more you drink, the more brave you become, and this night was no exception. Refueled and refreshed after our long day hiking, we were singing, dancing and having a blast. When Arron and Elaine left, the whole tone of the party changed. The atmosphere became more sexually-charged, more stimulating. My two guys friends—let's call them "Flip" and "Flap"—Mary and I began touching and kissing each other. Soon, all four of us ended up in bed.

At first, it was exciting but soon it became boring…if you can believe it. No one was willing to move it to the next level. We were stalled in halfhearted foreplay. Knowing that nothing else would happen, I decided to bring it to a stop. I said good-night to the guys and left. Mary soon followed. We were so exhausted from the hiking and carousing that we fell asleep in each other's arms. And the best part was that I didn't need a pillow—Mary's big, full, beautiful breasts were all the pillow I needed. I slept better than I had in years.

Chapter 5
Flashback, Flash Forward

My half-hearted 2013 New Year's resolution of being more relaxed and trying to avoid sex didn't last long. The next day, my usual dirty thoughts were plaguing me. I couldn't sleep, couldn't relax, on the bus ride back to New York. After a huge battle, I lost the fight with my libido and was aching to release my sexual tension. I was sitting alone near the front of the bus with my iPhone and headphones, watching porn. Luckily, everyone else was pretty tired, so no one bothered me. I don't think anyone else knew what I was doing. I was free to space out and get lost in my sexual imagination.

Before I'd left for Florida, my husband Apollo had gone back to Poland for a visit. My fantasies on the bus surprised me because they involved him. I knew I'd see him when I got back to New York. Since he left, I'd been having these wild erotic dreams while I slept, which always woke me up with a shattering orgasm. In fact, I had one of those dreams on my trip, while bunking with a woman in my tour group. I was too embarrassed to ask Alice if I made any noise when I came in my sleep. Had I woken her up with my dirty dreams? I'd never know.

A tour guide is like a gypsy, traveling from place to place, sharing rooms with strangers. It becomes my normal life. Any natural act that makes other people shy (like bathroom business) doesn't worry me at all. I find it funny to watch people try to hide everyday behavior. For example, they're afraid you'll hear them peeing or pooping the bathroom, so they put on the TV first, hoping it will cover the noise. (Usually it doesn't work, especially during the silences in a movie.) What a shame that people are so uptight and uncomfortable, even in the 21st century. You'd think we would have evolved further than that, worrying that our roommate might hear us using the toilet.

Even when I was younger, I felt the same way. In my high school religion class, I thought, 'If we're all brothers and sisters, why are we so ashamed of each other and of our bodies? We're supposed to be one, big, happy family, right? It makes no sense.

Sometimes I get envious of the indigenous people of South America or Africa. You know, the way they prance around happily, half naked, without inhibition. They're not afraid of showing their bodies. Often, they even decorate their bodies to make them even more attractive. They are free from the pitfalls of civilization and its barriers. They probably even don't even know what the word "taboo" means. So, why are modern people so closed-minded? I would love to show off my feminine beauty and my body, but I'm afraid I'd be ostracized or even worse, raped. This shouldn't happen in a big, happy family but ours seems to be a scared and dysfunctional one.

Look at me, after 10 days of traveling with the same people, sharing my time, bus, meals and bunking with them, I felt like we were family. But still, I needed to hide in the front seat with my porn instead of being up-front with them about my sexuality. Even I was a fraud.

The closer the bus got to New York, the more I thought about my husband Apollo. I knew he would be there, waiting for me to arrive in the home we shared. The irony was that he and I had gone on a trip like this to Florida two years earlier, in 2011. Apollo was the driver and I was the tour guide. We'd worked together three or four years, taking people on bus tours along the East Coast. Apollo was a work buddy to me—true, a super-handsome work buddy who was built like the Greek god Apollo (hence his nickname)—but nothing more than a business associate. Until we took that tour group to Florida, which changed everything.

I couldn't help but notice how good-looking Apollo was…it was impossible not to. At the time, I was dating Jenny, a beautiful Argentinean girl who happened to be in Florida for the Christmas holidays. We were planning on meeting there to celebrate New Year's Eve together but she ended up ditching me for some other girl. Pissed off, I decided to spend the first night of the New Year alone in my hotel room. I left my group around midnight and went straight to bed. The wall clock said it was ten after twelve. I'd already lost hope for a call from Jenny. The new year was going to suck, I decided.

Slowly, I stripped off my dress and put on my pajamas. Just then, the door opened Apollo walked in. (We not only worked as a guide team but we also shared a room for the whole tour.) Tall and well-built, Apollo had an uber-manly, macho demeanor. He looked at me gently with those cool, blue eyes, grabbed my wrist and pulled me closer for a kiss. "Happy New Year," I said, turning my cheek to him.

I was surprised when Apollo softly planted a kiss on my lips. "Here's to wealth," he told me.

"To wealth," I told him.

I was intrigued even though he looked like he'd been through the mill. This wasn't his best look—messy clothes, unshaven. It looked like he hadn't taken a razor to his handsome face for a few days. Apollo's stubble brushed my cheek when he kissed me. It felt like sharp knife points. He looked like a thief, not a lover. But I smiled at him anyway then went to bed.

As I closed my eyes, I was in a foul mood. Not the best way to enter a new year. Jenny, the girl I was hot for, was probably fucking someone else at that very moment and my driver, who I wasn't interested in, was hitting on me. I wanted to shoot myself!

For the rest of the trip, I did my best to ignore Apollo, even though people kept saying that we looked like a couple. I guess we acted like it. Besides sharing a room, we also shared food. I often fed him while he was driving, but it was no big deal. It all in fun. Remember, to me, life was just a source of amusement. Maybe I was ignoring reality because of my constant quest for the excitement that comes with pleasure. That was just the way I was built, so I accepted it.

There was one moment on that Florida trip when Apollo impressed me, though. So much so that I thought of being with a guy again. And that guy was him. It was a sudden impulse but a strong one. When I saw Apollo jump into the water to rescue a little dog who'd fallen down from the wall, I saw him in an entirely different light. Not only was he handsome and brave, but his act was a sign of deep caring and evidence that he had a good heart. At that moment, I realized that I didn't appreciate Apollo enough, and vowed to do better.

After seeing Apollo in full-blown hero mode, I figured, what the hell...why not go for it? I was single. My last date had ditched me. Arron was gone. What did I have to lose? I could give it a try with a guy again after years of being only with women. It was just a tiny thought and I tried to push it away. But for some reason, it wouldn't go. It just sat there, waiting for the right moment.

I liked Apollo as a friend and was afraid to ruin that relationship. Besides, I had a lot of possibilities waiting for me back in New York. The tour in Florida went on as it did before, despite the sweet kiss we shared. Nothing had changed between us but every so often, I thought of that kiss and couldn't help but wonder, 'What if?'

Apollo and I ended up becoming good friends. He was a great person, so kind and thoughtful. After some months, he had a proposition for me—we got along so well, why didn't the two of us move in together? It would save expenses and we wouldn't be alone. I thought about it long and hard. Even though I preferred women, Apollo and I had sex together every so often, and it was good, very passionate and loving. Something clicked between us. But Apollo also knew how I felt, that women were my thing, and he was fine with it. I knew he and I could be roommates because we bunked together as tour guides in Florida. So I agreed. Apollo and I moved in together. It worked out pretty well.

Soon after Apollo and I became roomies, my Visa was to expire. I didn't want to leave my new, beloved home and Apollo knew this. He asked me to marry him and I accepted. From the start, he knew where I was coming from. But one thing Apollo or I didn't expect was that he would grow to have deep, emotional feelings for me. Somehow, it happened, though. I didn't share the same type of feelings, although I loved him as a friend. I know it hurt him but I couldn't lie about something that just wasn't there. I cared about Apollo a lot, but not in the same way he did about me. He was okay with me being with women but didn't know that I also went other guys. I feel terrible about it now, betraying his trust. But I was a pleasure-seeker back then and would stop at nothing to get pleasure or adventure.

Looking back, I see what a big mess I made of things. I don't feel good about hurting Apollo. There's no other person like Apollo in my life but we're as different as two planets are. Just like planets exist together in the same solar system, Apollo and I are still in each other's orbit but soon needs to go away.

Fast forward to 2013. When I arrived in Brooklyn late from a Florida tour-guide gig, Apollo was waiting for me at home. (This trip was with another bus driver, not my husband.) I only had a few hours to repack before catching an early-morning flight to Buenos Aires and was planning on spending a few hours with Apollo, who I hadn't seen for about a month. On the whole two-day bus ride up from Florida, I imagined having amazing sex with him. I didn't expect anything else to happen but I was wrong. In New York, I've found that anything and everything can happen to anyone at any given time.

As soon as the bus got to New York, I received a text from one of my new Polish girlfriends. Beatrice said she just had to see me before I left for Argentina the next day. So many things had happened in her life during my trip to Florida that she needed to share with me. Besides, she missed me. Beatrice wanted to set up a dinner date for that night. I had very strong feelings for my new love, so I did as she asked.

After spending a couple of hours with Apollo, I headed out for a late dinner date with Beatrice. I picked her up at Limbo, the bar where she worked. Beatrice's beautiful, welcoming, smile gave me butterflies. I hadn't seen her for almost two weeks and really missed her. The previous four months, we spent almost every day in each other's company—bicycling, meditating, going out drinking together. So a couple of weeks apart seemed like an eternity. Beatrice and I made up for lost time. We wasted no time updating each other on what had happened in our lives during the time we'd been apart.

I was fully enjoying Beatrice's company, and my glass of Malbec, when the door opened and Jack walked in. A few days before my Florida trip, I spent my birthday kissing this beautiful African-American guy. There were big hugs and a few kisses from Jack, which I enjoyed immensely. But a little voice in my head was overwhelmed. 'Oh no,' it said. 'Not now! It's too much too soon!'

Beatrice's mood immediately changed when Jack started showering me with kisses even more kisses. Our ecstatic reunion immediately turned sour. I was really into Beatrice, not Jack—at least at that moment. And besides, my husband was waiting for me at home. I had promised Apollo I'd be back as soon as I could. Exhausted from my long bus trip, I wasn't emotionally prepared to handle all three of my love interests at once. Plus I only had a couple of hours before catching my crack-of-dawn flight to Buenos Aires. My life was turning into one of those romantic screwball comedies starring Julia Roberts!

I kissed Handsome Jack and apologized for what I was about to do—leave the diner with Beatrice. She and I found a quiet place and talked for hours. I wished I could stop time so she and I could steal away together for even longer. Things felt so comfortable and "right" with Beatrice that it seemed as though time sped up whenever we met. I felt sad that I couldn't give her the whole night she'd saved for me. Instead, I had to rush home to my husband.

Reluctantly, I drove Beatrice home. We ended up kissing passionately in my car. I tried to stop her, even though I desired her, knowing that we always ended up "making love" when we had a little bit to drink. At least we tried to have sex just for fun but sometimes we were so drunk, we never get very far.

Beatrice and I had already discussed our relationship earlier that night. We both agreed that we had to stop seeing each other as "lovers" because our relationship was going nowhere. (Even though I knew I couldn't stop it. Or maybe I didn't want to.) I returned Beatrice's kisses with as much passion as she kissed me with. Leaving her was difficult but I had no choice but to leave her on her doorstep. I finished the night with my husband and I fully enjoyed the short time we had together before I left him again.

My few hours back in New York were a whirlwind. And I was about to start another hurricane in the southern hemisphere.

Chapter 6
Up in the Air

Early the next morning, Apollo dropped me off at JFK airport. He wished me a good time in Argentina and I think he meant it. Although I was a little tired, I had beautiful memories from the night before. The 12 hours I'd spend up in the air en route to Argentina gave me plenty of time to think about the past year and scrutinize my life once again. I was determined to try and make sense of it. Apollo always told me that I looked into things too deeply, and maybe he was right. I was on a quest to get as much as I could out of life and I didn't want to waste precious time on things I shouldn't.

During my long plane ride, I couldn't stop thinking of the time I'd spent with my beautiful Polish girl, Beatrice. Even though she and I just talked, fooled around and kissed, I still couldn't get her out of my mind. How did it start, the whole flirtatious relationship between us?

I clearly remember the day Beatrice and I met. It was at a get-together for Polish women who love for traveling—and if you haven't guessed already, that describes me to a T. It was a beautiful June day in Greenwich Village. I'd originally planned to go to the meet-up with Mary, my Sugar Mama, but she begged out at the last minute so I went there alone. When I walked in, Beatrice was the first person I saw. The hostess for the event, she greeted me warmly, a bit more warmly than she greeted the others, I noticed. I was immediately attracted to her. Her gorgeous smile and deep, soulful eyes were enough to draw me in. I wanted to get to know her better. The meet-up was crowded and didn't last long but the first chance we had, Beatrice and I struck up a conversation. It turned out we had a lot in common, so we decided to meet again to pick up where we left off.

Busy, travelIng Polish ladies, Beatrice and I couldn't coordinate our schedules until a few months later. We met for dinner at Le P'tit Paris Bistro, a pretty French restaurant near Brooklyn's Prospect Park. It was a colorful New York autumn and still warm. The weather, the wine and pleasant talk had us feeling very comfortable with each other. I was even more curious about Beatrice and wondered if we would be as connected in bed. I hoped so.

Luckily, my attraction for my new friend Beatrice wasn't one-sided. It turned out that she was having the same vibes about me. We'd both admitted that we loved sex. Beatrice wasn't shy about telling me that she was bisexual. Maybe it was me or maybe it was the two glasses of Malbec we'd both had, but erotic matters were very natural and easy to discuss with Beatrice. Ah, Malbec...my favorite truth serum. It became our official companion for the rest of our relationship. Whenever she and I got together, so did Mr. Malbec, that sexy Argentinean from Mendoza.

The fact that Beatrice had opened up to me during our second meeting and declared her bisexuality to me so freely didn't really surprise me. I'd gotten the feeling she might be bi the moment I met her that night in the Village. But what really shocked me was that when I drove her home, I learned that Beatrice lived in the same building as my ex, Arron. My life seemed to be full of weird connections like this. I couldn't help but laugh out loud, and let Beatrice in on the little joke. Which was on me.

Beatrice also wasn't shy about telling me that when her last date dropped her off at home, the guy tore off her panties. Was it wishful thinking on her part? An invitation? I was a determined take thing slowly. I didn't feel ready to plunge headlong into another relationship. Maybe next time I'd rip off her panties, but not on the first date.

It was just before Halloween when I shared my first kiss with Beatrice. I remember this clearly because New York City was preparing for the arrival of Hurricane Sandy. And here I was, getting caught up in Hurricane Beatrice.

People didn't take the government warnings about what turned out to be Superstorm Sandy seriously. The weekend before it hit, they dressed up in costumes, went to parties and carried on as usual during the typical pre-Halloween festivities. Beatrice and I were no exceptions. I met my pretty Polish friend at a local bar. All of Park Slope looked like one big, vivid costume party. Everything from zombies to sexy nurses and nuns flooded the streets. I was one of them: decked out as a cowgirl, albeit a Polish one.

When I walked into Limbo, it was early but there were already a few people who, like me, arrived when it was less busy so they could get Beatrice's full attention before it got too crowded. (Or maybe I was just projecting my own feelings.) Since Beatrice started working there, the place always full with hopeful gentlemen (and ladies!) trying to pick her up. And I could see why.

Beatrice stood by the bar wearing a very sexy red dress that showed off her gorgeous figure. The dress had a plunging back and was cut down to the curve of her sweet, plump bottom, exposing lots of her creamy flesh. Beatrice smiled at me when I stepped up to the bar. I couldn't take my eyes off her. She was absolutely beautiful. I hoped this would be the night she and I would fall into bed together.

Beatrice and I spend a few hours drinking and chatting with the people around us. The crowd grew bigger every hour despite the threat of bad weather. The alcohol in my blood had warmed me up, made me braver. I wanted Beatrice even more. I felt lightheaded, both from the drinks and from my desire for her but I tried my best to stay sober. I wanted to have full control of myself just in case this would be our first time as lovers. A good, strong cup of coffoo put me right. Soon, we decided to leave the place. Together.

Except for a few caresses and exchanges of passionate looks, nothing happened between Beatrice and me at the bar. But I saw it as an invitation, a sweet preview to something that would soon happen between us. I tried my best to be patient, but Beatrice looked so lovely that it was tough. In the car, Beatrice played with my hand and fingers when I shifted gears. It was a gentle, sensual touch I hadn't experienced in a long time. I was lulled into a comfortable place and wanted more. But that's not exactly what I got. After all, it was close to Halloween, not Valentine's Day. Maybe that's why weird and wonderful things happened.

The coincidences between Beatrice and my ex, Arron, couldn't be ignored. My "first time" with Arron was on Halloween night. I took this as a hopeful sign for my budding romance with Beatrice. I smiled silently, fueled with more determination and confidence. 'Go for it,' I told myself 'Make a move tonight.' So, I kissed her. It was beautiful, intense, tender. The kind of kiss you don't want to end. It happened organically, naturally. But that's as far as it went. I wasn't disappointed, though, because that perfect kiss with Beatrice spoke of things to come. I felt strangely satisfied, like a conquistador. After dropping Beatrice off at her place, I went home and fell into a deep sleep in my husband's arms.

The next day was incredibly windy. Everyone was preparing for Hurricane Sandy, while I was still reeling from my kiss with Beatrice. Although no one knew it yet, Sandy would be the biggest hurricane in decades. The year before, there'd been warnings about another hurricane, Irene, which didn't turn out as bad as everyone predicted. (There was more damage in upstate New York from Irene, but not in Brooklyn.) Preparing for Irene the year earlier in 2011, I evacuated my apartment which was located in the least dangerous zone, Zone C. But I'd promised my mom I would evacuate, so I did.

To weather Hurricane Irene, I moved to my friend's house (this was before Apollo and I were roommates). I lived in the safe zone the night Hurricane Irene struck. I slept like a baby through it all, and the next day, I went back home like nothing had happened. On the way back to my place, I noticed that a few tree branches had come down, nothing more. So, when Sandy came to town, I ignored the storm panic. I spent the day cooking and enjoying being at home alone. My life, as usual, was a whirlwind so I really needed some down time.

The previous few weeks, besides flirting with Beatrice, I'd also been flirting with one of my coworkers at a community college where I taught part-time. I found Lola attractive long before Beatrice came into my life. Even though I didn't plan on flirting with Lola—isn't there an American saying, "You don't shit where you eat?"—there was always something I found very attractive about her. I decided just to play a little bit and see how far my dalliance with Lola went. I didn't hide my sexual preferences from her and Lola seemed to be game. She not only picked up on my flirtations but she flirted right back.

Lola admitted that she loved to flirt...with anyone. Later, she informed me that even though she was straight, she was bi-curious. So, here I was, saddled with yet another hetero honey was looking at bisexuality as a way to add a little spice to her life. But at least we were both on the same page and from the very beginning; I knew where Lola was coming from. In the end, nothing serious happened between us besides dirty games and sexting.

But during the hurricane, Lola came on strong...in her texts, at least. Yes, she and I were sexting each other during Hurricane Sandy. I wondered, did I have another storm on my hands besides Sandy and Beatrice?

When we were at work together, Lola asked me deeply personal questions about my sexuality which I tried my best to answer. I let the game continue and tried not to show all of my cards in the beginning. Like me, Lola seemed to enjoy "the chase." One day, she asked me the meaning of the Chinese letters tattooed on my arm. I told her that they were Chinese characters for energy, fire and harmony—the first two symbolized me, and the third was something I constantly sought. I asked if Lola had any tattoos. She did, but she made me guess its location on her body. The two on her inner wrists were a no-brainer but she had several more, she teased. The rest were in "private places," she admitted, leaving much to my imagination.

Our amusing sexting game continued as the winds became stronger outside. Although I didn't lose electrical power, I could tell that the storm was much worse than Irene the year before. There was a brief moment when I freaked out because I hadn't taken the storm as seriously as I should have. When the light blinked few times, I panicked. But since I was an adrenaline junkie, my heart beat faster because of the storm. Or was it because of the rising heat between me and Lola? If there was anyone to be stuck with during a hurricane, Lola wasn't a bad choice. Even if she was just on the other end of her cell phone and not there beside me. I couldn't ask Mother Nature for a better storm buddy.

With each crash of thunder I felt more paralyzed but it wasn't because of the hurricane, it was because of Lola. Actually, that's exactly what I was fantasizing about—I wanted to be paralyzed in a different way, helpless in Lola's arms. Being trapped inside my apartment while a violent storm raged outside was unbelievably thrilling. The desire rose furiously inside me, like the wind before thunderstorm, driving me toward total ecstasy. I began touching myself with abandon. My hands explored own body while the wind penetrated the city outside. Lola did the same on the other end of the line.

The storm grew more dangerous. My window frames shook and I was shivering, but not from been terrified but because my body was on fire. I was fantasizing about touching and kissing Lola. I could almost feel her hot hands and lips on my body. I let the sensation take over me. In a strange way, I felt united with hurricane raging outside. When the storm reached its peak, I did too, in an earth-shattering climax. I hope Lola did as well, safe at home in her own apartment. Satiated and exhausted, I went to bed with a big smile on my face.

The next day, I couldn't believe in the devastation Hurricane Sandy had caused. The East River had overflowed its banks. Downtown Manhattan, downtown Brooklyn, and even the train and car tunnels, were flooded. Many neighborhoods were without power. Parts of Staten Island were literally under water, and blocks and blocks in Breezy Point in Queens had burned down in a terrible fire. Hurricane Sandy was still raging beyond New York. It wreaked havoc in New Jersey and New England after it left us.

When I had the courage to go outside, my beloved Brooklyn was a wreck. Tree limbs and branches littered the sidewalks. Halloween decorations were strewn throughout the streets. My heart banged loudly in my chest when I went to check on my car. Along the way, I saw other cars with their windshields and hoods crushed with branches. Thanks God nothing happened to mine, not even a scratch. Many of my neighbors weren't as lucky. I felt a little bit guilty that while I was having an amazing orgasm, fantasizing about Lola, other people lost everything they had. It was karma, I tried to tell myself, the balance of good and evil. Something we had no control over.

Even though I was helpless over what had happened the night before, I realized that I could do something now. I jumped into my car and drove up and down the streets, looking for people who might need help. The streets were deserted. Later, I learned that almost everyone in Zone A, the area that sustained the most damage, were in dire straits. I didn't know where to begin. They needed basic things like food, water and clothes. The weather forecast didn't look promising for next few weeks. Each day looked worse than next, with the temperature threatening to dip way below freezing. I had to do something and it had to be quick.

I came up with the idea of collecting clothes from my friends to distribute to those who'd lost everything. As if reading my mind, my ex, Arron, called, asking if I wanted to volunteer to help Hurricane Sandy victims. It amazed me that even though she and I were apart, our minds were still in tune. Together, the three of us—Arron, her wife Elaine and I—headed out to the most devastated areas, the Rockaways and Breezy Point, with a car full of donations.

Dust and mud clogged the streets. Burned-down houses were everywhere. Plus it was dark because these places had no power. It looked like pictures I'd seen of cities destroyed during wartime. Dirty people with fear on their face seemed to be running everywhere yet were going nowhere. I felt their pain intensely and tried as much as I could to help. That day and later on as well. This had nothing to do with my "orgasm guilt." This went much deeper. I felt obligated to help my city, my new home, and its people. I put aside my foolish flirtation games. Helping out victims of Hurricane Sandy became the most important thing to me for the following weeks. Maybe this was the start of my metamorphosis, of my spiritual change, I thought. But actually, it would be a few more years until I became totally evolved.

I still had a long way to go. Even while I was helping out in the aftermath of the hurricane, I was dreaming about having a cocktail or two. A couple of days later, I gave in and met Beatrice, for a drink in Park Slope. After all the devastation I'd seen, I really enjoyed spending time with her. After a few cocktails, time—or the hurricane—didn't seem to exist anymore. Like party girls, Beatrice and I moved from one bar to another in Brooklyn Heights and Park Slope. We even considered inviting a guy to join us in a bed. I smiled at the thought of finally getting to make love to Beatrice—I didn't care if it meant sharing her with someone else. But the three way was only a crazy, drunken idea that never happened, leaving me with an empty sense of excitement and desire.

Without a male companion but still full of desire for each other, Beatrice and I moved to the next place. Bar Four in Park Slope was both cozy and animated, with live music and good alcohol. Everything seemed to be magical, as though Beatrice and I were players in a romantic movie, full of slow motion tracking shots and beautiful montages. Even the world slowed down. Our bodies moved to the same rhythm as we danced to the band, clutching each other. It was a totally euphoric moment. Beatrice and I couldn't resist. The temptation was growing in us and we started kissing passionately right there in the bar.

I don't remember exactly how it happened but we somehow ended up lying on the sidewalk outside of Bar Four. Beatrice was crying from the pain in her ankle. We thought it might be broken. (Thank God it wasn't!) People from the bar crowded around us, giving us bags of ice and bandages.

How did we go from ecstasy to sprained ankles? Did we go outside to get some air? Did we fall down while we were kissing? I vaguely remembered sitting down, caressing each other, then moving toward the exit. Had we stayed for one more song? Yes, we were leaning on the door and kissing. I don't know if someone else opened the door, but Beatrice and I went spilling out onto the sidewalk. If I thought hard, I could remember the sound of the menu board breaking under the crush of our bodies and Beatrice screaming loudly. This definitely woke me up from my erotic dream. Our beautiful night was officially over. It didn't end like I expected—in bed! —but it definitely ended our beautiful, little flirt. Taking that accident as a sign that we weren't meant to be together, Beatrice and I stopped dating and moved our relationship into the "Friendship Zone." Either way, it had reached a dead end.

I woke up with a splitting headache on my flight to Argentina. Too many difficult memories? Or was it from the airplane cabin's pressure? We'd hit a great deal of turbulence, which is probably what woke me up from my deep sleep and confusing emotions. I was working on very little rest since I had run back and forth between my girlfriend and my husband the night before. Plus, I had just arrived to cold New York from hot, sunny Florida. The temperature fluctuations, my intense night, air turbulence and altitude changes were probably too much for my body to handle.

For much of the long flight, I had traveled through my past, which was full of even more turbulence than the airplane, full of ups and downs, and emotional mayhem. I felt like I'd been through the wringer and I felt sick to my stomach. Maybe throwing up might actually help. I pictured cleaning out my stomach from the enormous amount of food and drink I'd had last night but also cleansing my soul from all of my sins. If I threw up everything—food, drink, past transgressions—maybe I could get absolution, forget about my screw-ups and start all over.

When I got up from my seat and was able to squeeze past my seatmates to use the bathroom, the turbulence came back again. All I could do was put my ass back in the seat, strap in again and weather the bumpy ride. I was lulled into a relaxed place by the pleasant, manly captain's voice telling the crew and passengers to prepare for landing.

The view of Buenos Aries from the window made me feel better. In moments, I forgot about my checkered past and looked ahead to a new future. Arriving in a brand new place for the first time, I left the "old world" behind. But where was my "old world," my haunting past? Was it in New York? In Florida? Or back in Poland? Just as I'd done in the US, I was running away from my complex life, aching to start another exciting episode in a different country. For a moment, I wondered if my old life and old problems would catch up with me in Argentina but I pushed those thoughts out of my head as soon as the plane touched down in Buenos Aires.

Chapter 7
First Tango in Argentina

Finally, my dream of visiting Argentina came true. It was on my bucket list as far back as I can remember. To a Polish girl, Argentina always seemed like such an exotic place. Maybe because it dangles tantalizingly at southernmost tip of South America. It's also thousands miles away from Eastern Europe, literally and figuratively. I was more than ready to encounter a lusty population of dark-skinned men and women, both in and out of bed.

As the airplane taxied on the runway, I grew even more excited. In a few minutes, I would be out and about in Buenos Aires. I couldn't wait to explore the country I saw through the little, round airplane window. I had a long list of places to visit all over this party town. Inside, I had the feeling that good things were waiting for me in this vibrant city of 10 million people. Someone exciting had to cross my way, I convinced myself.

Although thousands of miles away, I found Argentina to be more similar to Europe than I'd imagined. I discovered that many Argentinean natives are lighter-skinned than I was because of their northern European roots. Many of the Argentinean friends I had in New York had Italian or Spanish roots, so they tended to be more olive complexioned, but a good deal of those who settled in Argentina after World War II were of German descent, so they were much more pale-skinned.

Even the Spanish Argentineans spoke sounded different than the tongue of other Spanish-speaking countries. To my ear, the Argentinean accent has an Italian melody to it. The Argentinean attitude was a little snobbish, their look, a little European. It distinguishes them from the rest of the South American continent. Different in appearance and culture from its neighbors but still part of the South American world, I knew at once that I'd like it. Known for the tango and for the best steaks on the planet, I was thrilled to reach my long-sought-after destination.

Another reason I was excited to visit Buenos Aires was because I was invited there by my ex-lover, a sultry Argentinean miss named Jenny. Although she lives in New York part of the year, Jenny goes back home for the summer, which happened to be wintertime in New York. Memories of Jenny's hotness and my hate of snow and cold weather brought me to South American shores.

Jenny and I had met years ago, at a time when we both were going through big changes in our lives. The two of us had just ended long-term relationships and were in the process of discovering the "new us." Single ladies on the prowl, Jenny and I were open for any and every romance. We were also working on improving ourselves, better ourselves and trying to find the right place for ourselves in the world. I had a lot to learn—at the time, I thought I could "find" myself in someone else's bed. But I couldn't have been more wrong.

I suppose every woman goes through a transitional phase like that. Passing 30, with newfound independence, suddenly aware of her existence and her blossoming sexuality. That described me and Jenny to a T. We were different sides of the same coin. And we happened to "find" each other one night when I met another Argentincan friend for dinner. A friend of a friend, I found myself attracted to Jenny right away. I got the feeling that something would happen between us, and it did.

Jenny was exactly my type with a sexual energy that I sensed right off. It turned me on immediately. She had beautiful, smooth, café con leche-shaded skin, generous curves and a spark of vitality. Jenny popped into my life at the right moment. I was totally taken by her appearance and by her spontaneous personality. In a split-second, I forgot about my separation from my ex, Arron. (Arron who?) This sexy South American girl lifted this Eastern European's Iron Curtain, as well as my skirt. Jenny was to be my first sexual experience after a my seven-year relationship. My new sexual fascination and love for Jenny helped me pass through the darkest times of separation without tears and drama. I silently thank Jenny for that and for many other things as well.

Of course, the ride we took together was not without its bumps and bruises. With our very similar personalities Jenny and I understood each other, had a lot in common, but we also clashed. Since we had the same sort of energy and volatile temperaments, there were days when I felt like I was riding a rollercoaster—up, then suddenly unexpectedly and extremely down. Most days, we jogged together, still hung over after drinking and making love the night before. The enthusiasm and sexual stimulation would rise, and then, a very short time later, would fall when the realty of everyday life set in.

Our first "unofficial" date was in Ginger's, one of Park Slope's gay bars. It was in April, one of those gorgeous early spring days when everyone was out and about, seeking some fresh, warm air after an endless winter. The atmosphere crackled with sexual energy. Trees and flowers were bursting with life all around us and the feeling of blooming, of opening yourself up to the world, was unmistakable. I hadn't had sex for long time and felt erotically charged that day. Did I even remember the last time I made love with Arron? No, I didn't. My sex life was dead. It seemed like ages since anyone had even touched me. I wasn't sure if I still remembered how to make love to another person. I felt like a hungry animal in the middle of a barren desert. I missed tits, pussy and everything else that came with it.

At Ginger's, I found my Argentinean hottie sitting at the bar, sipping a glass of wine, chatting with other people. It was the first time Jenny and I were meeting without our friends around. We purposely didn't call it a "date" because we just wanted to find out how we'd relate to each other without the safety of our friends nearby. Jenny and I started out by talking nonsense instead of what was really on our minds: sex…love…lust. "How was your day?"Jenny wondered, like a bored housewife might ask her husband after his 9-to-5 stint at the office.

"Not bad," I told her. I wished I could think of something more witty to say but I came up empty. I was tired from long hours at my job. "I was working all day," I added. "I'm just glad to be here."

Jenny asked, "Have you been here before? Do you know this place?"

During my long relationship with Arron, we rarely went to bars. Although I was dying to go out, there was no need. I had everything I needed and wanted with Arron, who was not a "going out" type of person. Most of time, we just stayed home or invited people over. But I didn't want to tell Jenny this, so I responded, "Yes, I know this place. I've been here few times."

"Oh, I've never seen you at Ginger's before," Jenny responded, coolly. Damn, did she know I was lying? I was pretending to be someone I wasn't—a Playgirl, a confident seductress, and active lesbo. But the truth? I was rusty in the dating game and felt awkward as hell. But I didn't want Jenny to know that.

After our meaningless exchange, Jenny and I went down the laundry list that everyone covers on a first date. Even a first date that's not supposed to be a first date. Jenny and I were introducing ourselves to each other, trying to get comfortable with each other, but comfortable was the last thing I felt. After being with Arron for seven years, I didn't know what to do. So, I did nothing. First move? First kiss? Just thinking about it terrified me and the alcohol didn't help.

But the desire was there. I could tell that Jenny wanted me, too. Brave cowards, neither of us made the first move at Ginger's. We kept the conversation light and breezy, staying in the safe Friendship Zone. Neither of us was clear on whether this was actually a date or not. Despite our attraction to each other, both of us didn't have balls—or clits, since we were bi—to make it more obvious than it was. On top of everything, the bartender inserted herself into our conversation. Was it my imagination or was she flirting with Jenny and me at the same time?

Paralyzed with fear, I wasn't prepared for the single, gay world out there. Or the games Jenny and I played later on. Right before my eyes, I lost the lady I'd been so excited about. I couldn't believe it when the bartender ended up with my Argentinean dream girl. I was so upset that I decided not to give up and fight over Jenny instead. Sure, it was a challenge and I loved every part of the chase. Even if I lost Jenny to the pushy bartender, I planned to put up one hell of a fight. Maybe that was part of Jenny's game—to get my attention and fight for her. But I knew that sooner or later, she was going to be mine. It was clear there was a strong chemistry between us, no matter how scared I was of dating.

Every time Jenny and I met, there was an undeniable sexual energy in the air, even though we kept it in the Friend Zone…at first. We partied a lot, determined to have the best summer in the city. At times, I felt like an actress, playing a role in that TV series The L Word. And for the first time in a long time, I felt good, sexy, desired, and finally free. Just like those girls in the Showtime series. I felt new, awesome and fresh. I'd finally left Arron and our dead relationship behind. I was fully enjoying the gay community.

The erotic atmosphere around us... the sexual desire in Jenny and me was rising quickly. We went out a lot together and had a blast clubbing in Brooklyn, Manhattan and even out of town. In between a trip to that gay Mecca, Fire Island, and gay bars, Jenny and I finally kissed. It was early in the morning with the first bird's song on the background, very romantic.

Jenny and I had spent the evening before together, but we never slept. In fact, we were up all night. Together, Jenny and I never once stopped moving. We were an energetic force to be reckoned with. Either we were bowling or drinking our way through Williamsburg. Tipsy and totally into each other, we couldn't resist the temptation anymore. We left the last bar of the night, having maxed out our credit cards. It was already morning. Although we were broke, Jenny and I were still flirting with each other heavily and hesitantly touching each other. Our bodies drew closer and closer. Time seemed to stand still. Still playing, with me and with words, Jenny whispered, "I won."

The feel of her warm breath against my ear, my neck, was driving me crazy with wanting. "But only because I let you win," I told her.

Jenny laughed. What a beautiful smile she had, what perfect teeth. I wanted to run my tongue along them. "You're lying," Jenny told me. "You had too much Jack and couldn't hit the bowling pins."

I wouldn't let Jenny get the upper hand. With a little arrogant smile on my face, I said, "It's because you kept distracting me all night long."

Jenny's smile disappeared and her face became serious. She gave me this deep, solemn look that silently said, 'Take me.'

In response, I immediately became wet. I knew this was the right moment. I pulled Jenny close, our breasts pressing against each other. The time was right. I finally kissed her, and she kissed me back. I felt reborn in my old skin. Brave, like I could do anything. The old Maggie had resurfaced after such a long absence, after disappearing somewhere along the way, Maggie was back.

But I still wasn't home free with Jenny. I learned that Bartender Girl, from Ginger's, was still actively pursuing her. Jenny reluctantly admitted that they were dating and it drove me crazy. If Bartender Girl was so great, then why was Jenny still messing around with me? I had a feeling their relationship would end soon. I wanted to make sure I was around when it did and so I could finally get Jenny's full attention. I didn't care about Bartender Girl's feelings—I didn't think too much about other people's feelings or karma back then. All I cared about was my feelings about Jenny. All that mattered was to have her.

The apocalypse arrived one day toward the end of that summer. Jenny, Bartender Girl, some friends and I went to Staten Island to play paint ball. Hot-looking girls with weapons in hands and dirt on their faces was a huge aphrodisiac for me. Hiding behind trees, crawling through the dirt hunting for each other, looking aggressive but attractive... Despite being aroused, I so wanted to kick Bartender Girl's ass. Yes, I was jealous and willful, especially with the paintball gun in my hand. I did my best to knock out Bartender Girl with my paintball bullets. She was splattered with colors all over her jumpsuit, but then again, so was I. But I think she realized that I was out for the kill

The next day, I couldn't move. My whole body hurt. My soft, delicate skin was covered with huge purple circles from being hit with paintballs. Bartender Girl and me had gotten the worst of it. But not from each other—it was from Jenny. My Argentinean dream girl took advantage of both of her love interests. Bartender Girl and I were so smitten with Jenny that we couldn't shoot her up with paint. Jenny, on the other hand, had no problem shooting the crap out of us.

Maybe I lost the paintball battle, but I won the war. Soon after, Jenny informed me that she'd broken up with Bartender Girl. I was thrilled to hear this but a little part of me was afraid. Could I keep up with Jenny's insane energy? Could I keep her happy? Could I keep her from getting bored?

In our flirtatious games, Jenny and I had both run on an adrenaline for the past few months. I knew I couldn't keep up that pace. But even exhausted from lack of sleep and too much alcohol, a magic fuel kept us going, gave us the feeling that nothing could stop us. (Was it lust?) Whatever it was, Jenny and I were inexhaustible. We participated in our first 5K race. We signed up for climbing and kickboxing classes, and we were learning how to ride motorcycles. Jenny and I also volunteered at an organization called Lifebeat. Together, we gave away free condoms at events and live concerts. We got to hang out with all sorts of cool people. Looking back, 2010 was my best summer in New York City.

Jenny and I seemed to be charged by the same Energizer Bunny battery but the roller coaster ride that was us also needed to regenerate. During our quiet moments, we both focused on ourselves. Escaping to yoga and meditation, Jenny and I were constantly analyzing the mistakes we'd made, trying our best not to repeat them. We still connected deeply on a physical level but we also made an effort to try and understand each other and build a strong relationship. We weren't very successful at the "understanding" aspect of our union because we weren't 100% honest with each other. I guess we were afraid of the feelings we both had for each other. That's how deep and intense they were.

For a long time, we categorized our relationship as "friends with benefits," never as lovers. I wish it could have stayed that way but my feelings betrayed me. Jenny and I shared incredible, spontaneous dates that always involved lots of wine and wild sex. I just didn't know how to express my feelings properly. That was my big mistake. Maybe it was the language barrier between us— Polish was my first language and Spanish was hers, while we communicated in English, a foreign tongue for us both. Instead of trying to share our emotions, we kept everything inside and covered it up with alcohol and orgasms.

But our sex life...it was spectacular. One time, Jenny and I were on the New Jersey cliffs that overlook the Hudson River, with the Manhattan skyline just across the river. We opened a bottle of wine, drank, talked and felt very close to nature—and each other. A second bottle of wine was opened in Jenny's backyard. We easily left reality and became lost in a world of erotic imagination. Kissing, playing with each other's hands and fingers, it was a huge turn-on.

The pop of a champagne cork transported me to another place. I remembered a time when it was more than just Jenny and me. In my mind's eye, I pictured Jenny and me making out on my living room floor and my male roommate suddenly walking in on us. He still thanks me to this very day for the best love scene of his life—having two girls making love to him at once, every man's fantasy.

Another time, Jenny and I went to a swingers' meet up after we attended a contemporary piano concert. What a contrast! After the downtown concert, we ended up in a posh apartment on the Upper East Side near Central Park. A friend of Jenny's had invited us. When Jenny asked if I wanted to go with her,

I told her, "Sure, I'll give it a try. I've never been to a get-together like that." I was always looking for adventure back then.

"You don't have to do anything if you don't want to. Just tell me and we'll leave." I had a feeling Jenny had been to parties like this before, and more than once. My curiosity got the best of me. Was Jenny testing me?

I paused for a moment. "Well...I like to try new things but it doesn't mean I'd like this." Then I added, "But let's go check it out." I was waiting for Jenny to respond. Maybe she was calling my bluff and then would say she didn't want to go when I said I did. But instead, we went inside to the party.

When we arrived, I was surprised to see that the apartment was almost empty of furnishings. There was hardly any furniture and it smelled like it had been freshly painted. There were a few sofas, a couple of beds and a television. Plus lots of alcohol odd-looking people scattered throughout the cold, three-bedroom apartment.

I couldn't seem to find my own space or feel comfortable. I did my best to look cool but I don't think it was working. It was another "life experience" to chalk up to the rest, I told myself. I wasn't obligated to do anything. As I did a quick visual scan of the room, I found no one even remotely interesting or the least bit good-looking. Except for Jenny.

Chills ran down my skin when one of the older couples at the sex party just walked up to me and started touching me. No introduction, no nothing. They just began pawing me. Scared to death, I bolted, and began pushing Jenny toward the door. She looked at me with disappointment on her face but knew I was horrified. "Let's get out of here," she said reluctantly.

In order to exit, we had to pass through two rooms of people making out, in various stages undress. There were three, four, five of them piled up together. I'd never seen a big orgy face-to-face and it was gruesome. The animalistic grunting noises, the unattractive people...it was all too much for me. The horrible picture of gross bodies rutting haunted me for weeks, like a nightmare. I was thoroughly disgusted. I couldn't think of sex, even sex with someone as beautiful as Jenny. I had a vision of demigods making love to each other in a hedonistic celebration, something that might have taken place in ancient Greece. Instead, I was confronted with a sexual freak show, which like a horror film.

Arriving in Buenos Aires, I vowed to leave these memories far behind. I tried to focus on Jenny and the new adventures we might encounter. I went through immigration without a problem and entered a new world, leaving the sad orgy, my husband, Beatrice, Jane and everyone else, far behind.

Waiting for me at the airport were Jenny, and her friends Anita and Rita. They were the type of lesbian couple who seemed like they'd always been together—and always would be together. Rita, the younger one, looked me up and down. Even after a 12-hour flight, it seemed that she approved of me. I was young, Eurotrash, newly-arrived from the gay paradise that was New York. Fresh meat. Rita and I didn't know it yet, but she would soon be my lover. Her 17-year relationship with Anita was in crisis, and meeting me didn't help. Little did I know that they hadn't had sex for many months and Rita was ripe for the picking.

I had only been in Buenos Aires a short time and I was loving it. Beautiful women were everywhere you looked. I was immediately intrigued by another girl who arrived at our place late that night. Quiet and mysterious, she got my attention even after 24 hours without sleep. I talked to this nameless girl for a few minutes, seeking a meaningful connection. After my long monologue to her, everyone laughed. It seemed that Pretty Girl (aka Lana) couldn't speak a word of English. Besides that, she wasn't interested in me, but in Jenny, who'd left her current girlfriend behind in New York. Disappointed and exhausted, I left them all and went to bed.

After few hours of sleep, I was awakened by the incredible heat. I was literally soaked in sweat. I would soon learn that January is the worst time of year to visit Argentina. People leave Buenos Aires in droves looking for a cooler place to spend the summer. (Kind of like Paris in August, only way hotter.) I never experienced this intense kind of heat in New York. Coming from the chilly climate of Eastern Europe, I love heat, but not heat this intense. I had a huge headache and I hadn't even gotten out of bed yet. With the high temperatures and lack of sleep, I felt dizzy nauseous and still drunk. The welcoming champagne I'd had the night before was sour in my stomach. I felt exhausted and ill.

I'd just put my body through the gauntlet, temperature-wise, and now it couldn't seem able to adjust. In last few days I'd traveled from warm Florida to the frigid New York winter and back to hellishly hot Argentina. Still in shook, I didn't even know where I was anymore or why I was here. Oh, right...Jenny.

I was here in Buenos Aires trying to rebuild my friendship with Jenny. After few months of silence, she and I began communicating again and I really enjoyed it. After my relationship with Arron crumbled, I was eager to see if things could start back up again with Jenny. What better way to do this than to jump right in and visit her. Stranger things have happened. Still tired but excited, I was ready to rock and roll. I put myself together, shook off my hangover and made up my mind to conquer Buenos Aires.

On my list for the day was a trip to La Boca, a funky neighborhood known for Caminito, which was a street full of colorful houses and bohemian art galleries. I loved the old buildings painted electric blues, greens and yellows. It was like a Crayola crayon box come to life. On every corner were sexy dancers giving tango lessons for few Argentinean pesos. All around, people were dancing and laughing. We found a nice restaurant in a section that reminded me of Williamsburg in Brooklyn. Along with me and Jenny were her friends Anita and Rita, who made us laugh with stories about Rita's twin sister, who was also gay, and their brother, who was a priest. It was a nice balance, a good beginning. Right from the start, we all felt comfortable with each other. There was no shallow conversation but talk that went deep.

Yes, I was loving Argentina and getting to know this exciting country. A few days after I arrived, we hosted a techno house party and things took a different direction. Meaning, they spiraled out of control. We rented all of the equipment including huge speakers, laser and smoke machines. Feeling like teenagers, we were pumped by music, lights, heat and weed. I felt like I was going to explode with tension, sexual and otherwise. We all were feeling same way. Something in the air, maybe. The summer heat had everyone looking for adventure. Or it could have been too much gay, female hormones condensed into one small space.

I don't remember what pushed me to do it but I soon found myself kissing Jenny's friend, Rita. Luckily, Rita's much-older partner Anita wasn't into techno parties and decided to stay home. I'm a bad girl, I know. I tried to resist my impulses but I couldn't. (And why should I, I told myself, I was on holiday.) Rita kissed me first but I didn't reject her advances. Instead, I kissed her back with even more intensity.

In between kisses, Rita tried to convince me that her relationship with Anita was already over. "It's just a matter of time," she said. I felt guilty but also incredibly turned on. Finally, had a real lesbian, not a straight girl who was bi-curious. I was tired of dating straight girls. Recently, my sexual liaisons were limited to my husband and straight girls. How pitiful was that? With straight girls, you never knew what they wanted and neither did they. You couldn't count on having anything more than just nice flirt. How frustrating. Basically, besides innocent kisses, all you get is drama. And I was tired of drama.

With lesbians it's different. There's still drama, but a different kind of drama. From the beginning you get a gut feeling whether it's going to work out or not. You know what you want and you go for it right away. There are no games, no false pretenses. You know where you're heading and the answer is easy, either "yes" or "no." And with Rita, the answer seemed to be yes, yes, yes. But then there was the matter of Anita. I pushed her out of my mind for the moment.

It's no secret how Argentineans love their meat, and lesbians are no exception. The next day, Jenny, Rita and I went for a grill party out of town. Guess where? At Rita's partner Anita's house. I felt awful. No words could describe it. Anita had no clue what had happened the night before between me and Rita. I felt so evil. Especially because Anita was happy to have me for as a lunch guest. She was a gracious hostess, which made things even worse.

Looking back, I can't help but wonder what the hell I was doing back then. My thoughts were only primal—sex, food, and creature comforts. I didn't think about how my actions would affect other people. I only looked at what I wanted and needed. And now!

Anita not only cooked for all of us but offered to let me take a nap in her bed. Yes, the famous siesta South America is famous for. I swallowed hard and didn't know what to do. Shame on me, I thought. In my next breath, I tried to forget about everything that had happened with Rita the night before. In front of Rita, no less, I was pretending that there was no yesterday. Deep inside, I knew I was lying to myself but I ignored it. Back then, I was good at ignoring the truth. I learned how to easily forget the past and convince myself that nothing bad had happened, to wipe it out from my memory like it never even existed. I was emotionless, accepting things just the way they were on the surface. Careless, I did bad things without looking at the consequences. But deep inside I think I knew that one day karma would come back and bite me on the ass.

It's funny how mankind can be so harmful, so self-destructive. It's a disease from which we all suffer. At some point, I felt like I deserved it. I was still carrying around the guilt I had after my seven-year relationship with Arron. I felt like I had screwed it up and now had to punish myself by getting into a string of meaningless relationships that went nowhere. This, in turn, made me become a proverbial "bad girl." I had to let out everything that was inside me. Maybe then I would finally begin to heal. I was going crazy, partying left and right, fucking every girl I could, whether or not they were in relationships. I was full of emotions but none of them good. In the meantime, I was hurting myself and the people all around me.

But why was I acting out like this? And why did I magically appear in Rita's life when her relationship was falling apart? Was I the devil who causes the breakup or the angel who saves the damsel in distress? I didn't want to answer that question.

For the time being, I was still enjoying my stay in Buenos Aires, filling myself with pleasure every moment I was there. Dancing, drinking, drugging. I couldn't get enough.

A friend of Jenny's in Palermo had recommended a wonderful yoga studio so Jenny, Rita and I decided to check it out. I think it was the first step on my path to enlightenment. This wasn't just any yoga studio. It was incredible, beyond our expectations. In a private apartment with a huge balcony, Buddha statues decorated every corner and yoga mats were scattered across the floor. Beautiful Oriental plants filled the balcony, spreading their intense aroma throughout the room. It was perfectly arranged and had a strong spiritual atmosphere. I couldn't ask for more. I was so impressed, it made me dizzy.

The calm, gorgeous yoga instructor immediately introduced us to her spiritual secret. Laughing, she took us to the kitchen and opened the refrigerator. "It's hot today," she said. "Do you want some refreshments?" I was in the mood for a tall drink of something cold, but that's not what I got. The entire refrigerator was stuffed with marijuana. Tons of it. 'Well, that explains her calmness,' I thought to myself.

"Why not!" all three of us said at the same time. I wasn't really a pot person but I longed to be as serene as the yogi was. Between her beauty and her relaxed behavior, I was attracted to her. She was slim, had a nice smile, skin and hair. But there was something more about her. She seemed to shine from within. I longed to be like that. I wanted to feel and look as good as she did. But I had a suspicion that her demeanor was more than the pot, more than just yoga stretches. I think she was fulfilled on all levels.

It turned out to be one of the best yoga classes of my life. The language barrier wasn't a problem to me at all. I don't speak Spanish but stoned, I felt like a skilled polyglot. Although I was probably mixing all of the languages I knew into my speech, I didn't care. The marijuana got rid of my inhibitions.

After the yoga class, a bunch of us went to a queer tango party. When in Argentina, you've got to tango, right? This one was very unusual in that it was hard to distinguish between the dancing bodies who was male and who was female. We all moved together as one, all mixed up. But somehow, it all worked. We were beautiful and free in our movements, or maybe it was just my perception, still being stoned from the yoga studio.

The tango dance hall was dimly lit, mysterious. Would someone jump out from the corners, rob us, or worse? But I tried to push the paranoia from my mind, just go with the flow and not think. We danced with girls, boys, and everything else in between. I'd have someone in my arms who first appeared to be a guy but turned out to be a girl. Then I was dancing with (and kissing) my sweet Rita again. Then it was Jenny once more. What a beautiful, free-flowing evening it was.

At first, I was leading Rita on the dance floor, then Jenny took the lead. I let her strong personality overtake me, enjoying the slow, sensuous movement of the tango. It felt odd. Looking straight into Jenny's eyes, I got goose bumps. My memories of her flooded back, the excitement and incredible time we had together in New York. A series of lovely movie clips played in my mind. I journeyed between the past and the present, between New York and Argentina. I knew the romance between Jenny and me was over. We were friends now and we were both clear on that point. And more importantly, we were both okay with it. So many things had changed since New York.

Once or twice, I had to fight the brief and spontaneous romantic feelings about Jenny that bubbled to the surface. I shook them off and turned to Rita, my new dance partner. "Can we please go somewhere else?" I begged. "This is all too much for me to deal with in one night."

Without hesitation, Rita replied, "One day at a time. Don't worry, I'll take you home." But where was home? I was adrift, apartment-hopping in a new country. I stayed with whatever friend was kind enough to take me in for the evening.

A few minutes later, I found myself at Rita's mother's house. Like many Argentineans, Rita's mom went out of town for the summer, and Rita had full run of the house while her mom was gone. Feeling like teenagers doing forbidden things in the master bedroom, Rita and I made out in her mother's bed. It was sinful, wonderful.

Another evening, Jenny and I visited a gay hotel called the Axel in the Palermo section of Buenos Aires. It was gorgeous, made all of glass: glass elevators, stairs, walls and floors. You could see all the way up and down the building, even to where the glass swimming pool was. In the restaurant on the first floor below, you could see swimming bodies above you as you ate and drank. All you had to do was tilt your head up while you were enjoying dinner.

Jenny and I went to the Axel for supper and to talk. We both felt the need to tie up the loose ends from our past. Finally, we'd learned to talk instead of yell or bottle up our feelings inside, but it was too late to salvage a romantic relationship. We both agreed about that. There were still some issues to be solved and we really tried. At least Jenny and I both admitted that we'd made lots of past mistakes but we also discovered that we'd learned from them. Jenny and I promised we wouldn't repeat them. Once more, we agreed that we were better as friends than as lovers. We'd grown a lot and were now able to move on to the next level. Jenny and I left yesterday behind and trusted the universe. We were ready to conquer the world now that we'd conquered our past transgressions against each other.

Our courage and candor was probably attributed to the two bottles of wine we consumed during dinner. To make the night more memorable, some of our friends arrived to surprise us. A good excuse to order another two bottles of wine.

Basically, we all took over the Axel: a few sweet gay boys, Jenny, Rita, myself and Pretty Girl/Lana, who always kept popping up. The place belonged to us, since nobody else was there. We decided to stay the night at the hotel. We couldn't resist the tempting swimming pool, among other things. We soon learned that the Jacuzzi and pool were reserved for VIPs and special guests, which we were not. We had to use all of our collective charm and skills of persuasion to convince the handsome receptionist to let us into the pool area. It didn't take long. He gave us a quick tour and set the rules. But he was the first one to break the rules when he abandoned his post at the front desk. All it took was a few minutes of nice conversation with us before he decided party with us instead of going back to work.

I was the first one to take off my clothes off and go naked into the Jacuzzi with a bottle of wine, breaking Rule # 2 and # 3 (No alcoholic beverages in the Jacuzzi and no nudity.) Feeling a little tipsy and very liberated, I was fully enjoying the sensation of the bubbles massaging my skin. The other women soon followed me. Their lovely, little drunk faces reflected the happiness we all shared at that moment. We didn't care about anyone in the restaurant down below seeing us. We just enjoyed being naked, drunk and a little high on weed. The heat of the Jacuzzi and the effects of alcohol worked their aphrodisiac magic on me. I felt warm inside and out, filled with desire. I tried to cool my libido down by jumping into the pool's cold water but it didn't help.

Still hot and high, I imagined myself a sensuous fish or a lusty mermaid. I pictured the four of us girls as Aphrodites with and one Neptune, the male receptionist, who jumped in right after us. Naked, we all clutched each other's slick, shimmery skin. The glowing swimming pool, with its dim green and blue lighting, helped heighten my imagination. Between the beautiful bodies, the ambiance and my desire, I was incredibly aroused. The temperature inside me rose quickly and grew to such a high level of heat that I felt I could have an orgasm right there, without anyone touching me. The ecstasy of the moment and being skin to skin with my summer girl, Rita, took hold of me. We soon moved to a room and the rest of the night was intense, fiery.

A few hours later, the bright sunlight woke me up. The sun was everywhere and refused to let me sleep. A totally-glass hotel is great in theory, and at night, but during the day, it isn't conducive to sleeping! There was nowhere to hide. Everywhere I turned, the sun followed me. It reflected off the mirrors, off everything. Exhausted, I tried to dig myself a cave made of pillows. My soft, fluffy castle seemed to work and I looked forward to getting a few more hours of blessed sleep. But when I turned on my side, I felt something sticky—I was lying on a small pile of chocolate and strawberries from the night before.

Besides that, I had another huge hangover. When I stood up and surveyed the room, I saw that I was alone. Rita—and everyone else—was gone. I couldn't believe that she'd left me alone in this strange and wonderful city of 10 million people...just because she had to get to work. I had no idea where I was. Disoriented and with a headache that would kill a lesser woman, I discovered that I'd maxed out my credit card. I had no money, spoke no Spanish and had chocolate all over my clothes. But the memory of the night before put a smile on my face. I pulled myself together and headed out onto the streets of Buenos Aires, alone, but ready to face whatever life was about to throw in my path.

Chapter 8
New York State of Mind

My trip to Buenos Aires passed quickly and before I knew it, it was time to return to my jumbled life in New York. Not that my life in Argentina was any less of a jumble! The reflection of the world below through the little airplane window looked so barren and uninviting. As we landed in JFK Airport, I noticed that the trees were covered with snow. Just five p.m., it was already dark and I felt a shiver of coldness rush through my body. My long, sunny days in Argentina were over. I consoled myself with thoughts that New York would be my temporary stop before escaping again to who knows where. I had an unquenchable thirst for travel, almost as strong as my thirst for sex.

At some point, I knew I had to get back to reality, which I'd left behind only a few weeks earlier. I escaped to reboot my life and now I was ready to face my problems and get things in order once and for all. Or was I? I tried to console myself with thoughts that springtime would soon be upon us. It always feels so hopeful because that's when everything blossoms and comes back to life. If the Earth could renew itself, then so could I. I truly believed this.

The frozen world before me frightened me; it held so many unanswered questions. It surprised me that I was looking forward to seeing my husband Apollo. What strange emotions and realizations! For a lesbian like me to miss her husband, or even have a husband in the first place is odd in itself. But I missed Apollo's strong arms around me, his body, the scent of his skin.... the sex. I also missed the feeling of being protected by him, knowing that I was being watched over and that I was safe and secure. I let my guard down a bit with Apollo, and allowed myself to feel to love. And it felt good.

Apollo was a comforting thought, especially returning to New York City on ice. The entire East Coast was locked in the midst of a polar vortex in February 2013. It was nice to know that at the tip of the iceberg, there was someone who loved me, wanted me, needed me, and was waiting for me.

The air outside at JFK was frigid. I put on my gloves and wrapped myself in my heavy down winter jacket before stepping into the cold, night air and into the next chapter of my life. After the heat of Buenos Aires, New York seemed unfriendly and bitter cold. I took in my surroundings slowly, my eyes tearing from the icy blast, when I spotted him. My husband. And who was there beside Apollo, but Beatrice, my Polish beauty. She was shivering like a puppy and jumping in place to stay warm. Two people I cared deeply for were anxiously awaiting my arrival, scanning the faces in the swarm of people coming and going, and greeting loved ones. I supposed I was their loved one.

Covered up in the cocoon of my down jacket, Beatrice and Apollo still hadn't recognized me, even as I walked toward them. I suddenly stopped. I needed a moment to process all of this. Every time I think life can't possibly surprise me more, it does. How is it that Beatrice and my husband have finally met and both of them are here at the airport to retrieve me? I struggled with my emotions as I tried to figure out which one I was happier to see. Both Beatrice and Apollo were so dear to my heart in such very different ways. Or were they just the same?

In a flash, I had a crazy thought. I could pull my collar up higher, turn around and leave, without them even recognizing me. I could be a coward as I have been many times in the past and just run away. I could take my bags, the money in my pocket and just board the next plane to anywhere. But then I reminded myself that I wanted to come back to New York and work things out. But slowly, not bombarded by my two loves the second I stepped off the plane.

I took a deep breath and shook off my thoughts of fleeing. I decided to jump in with both feet and go for it. With a big smile on my face, I ran right up to my husband and ladylove, and threw my arms around them both. All three of us hugged before we ran to the car, excited and freezing. Once inside, Apollo blasted the heat as we tried to warm up. Touched that they had a bottle of champagne waiting, I softly kissed my husband's cheek and grabbed Beatrice's hand. It was heaven. Yes, it was good to be home. All the doubts and fear I had moments before were replaced by the warmth of friendship and love, and being with two people I cared about deeply. But who would I spend the night with?

After two glasses of champagne, I decided to play the good wife and go back home with my husband. Exhausted, I collapsed into bed not feeling a thing but contentment.

Waking up next day in to the gray New York City winter light glaring through my windows, I felt pain throughout my body. There were bug bites all over my beautifully tanned skin and blood on the sheets. A cold chill took over my body. Did I have a fever? 'What the hell?' I thought to myself and jumped out of bed. I pulled back the sheets and to see them covered with bedbugs. "Fuck, no way!" I screamed. Was I being punished for all of my dirty sins in Argentina?

Bed bugs. The scourge of the city. What a way to be welcomed back when the night before had so much promise. I was too tired and too upset to try and figure out how this had happened. Did I bring back the bedbugs from Buenos Aires? Did I get them on the airplane? Was it the man I rented the apartment to? Apollo and I traveled so often, we could have gotten them anywhere. All I knew is that it was 6 am, dark and freezing cold. After Apollo and I called an exterminator, he forbade us to return to the apartment for another 10 or 12 hours because of the fumigation. Where was I going to go?

An overnight snowstorm had covered the frigid Brooklyn streets with inches of thick, white powder. The neighborhood seemed paralyzed by the storm. Everything was closed. There were no stores or coffee shops to sit in and relax in. On top of that, I felt abandoned by my friends who were afraid to let us stay with them because of the bedbugs. Of course, I understood but it still hurt. One of my best friends, Anna, told me point blank, "I'm sorry. I love you, girl, but no way are you going to bring that shit to my place!"

Unwelcome anywhere, I had no idea where to go. Should I take a long drive? I still felt feverish. I also felt no hope, that there was no bright side to the situation at all. I knew I was being punished. For what? For being a hedonist? For loving life? Maybe that in itself was a sin.

Depressed as I was in the dark, cold winter, I still searched for something to keep up my spirits. I couldn't seem to adjust to the weather and the harsh reality of New York City. Looking for peace of mind, I turned to something that had recently given me solace: yoga and meditation. Beatrice was happy to accompany me to a yoga center I'd recently discovered in Manhattan.

Despite all of my drinking, carousing and fooling around, I was still on a quest for enlightenment. I just got side-tracked every so often. More and more, people I came across inspired me to do better, to try harder in my search for my true self. In this, my "Christ Year," I was looking for the true me and having a hard time unearthing her. I was my own worst enemy, though, because I kept repeating my negative behavior patterns. But I was also eager to change and willing to observe myself.

The biggest thing I needed to learn was how to distinguish between sex and friendship, and to stop being led around by my primal sex urges. I hoped that like Dante in The Divine Comedy, after going through Hell and Purgatory, I would finally arrive at Heaven. At least that was my belief. My Polish Beatrice was like Beatrice, Dante's afterlife guide who took him on his soul's journey for a deeper level of spiritual understanding. I imagined that my Beatrice was doing the same thing for me, but not in the afterlife, in present-day New York.

I was on the path to change and enlightenment. I was learning how to meditate, which was not an easy task for an energetic person like me. Each time I closed my eyes, pictures of me misbehaving played in my mind's eye. I couldn't find answers to the things that were bothering me. At first, meditation didn't help me in piecing the broken parts of my life together as it does for some. I find it incredibly difficult to sit still and clear my mind. It made me anxious and antsy, so I decide to take a break and try meditation again when I was more calm and in the right headspace for it.

Although taking a journey to find the inner "us" and looking for solutions from within didn't bring Beatrice and me the results we were expecting, it brought us something to else instead: sex.

One day, before a private meditation session, Beatrice pulled something out of her trendy purse. When I took a closer look, I noticed that it was a huge green dildo. Not very Zen or conducive to meditation. Extremely elastic, it could easily move from side to side like a tree branch swaying in the breeze. Supposedly, it was exactly a shape and length of a famous journalist's penis. "Maggie," Beatrice said breathlessly. "You should try it on for size so at least you get the sense of having him in your pussy."

"Well, I don't know if that's what I'm dreaming about, but okay," I told her. "Let me give it a shot."

As I took the Green Giant from Beatrice, I wondered silently, 'Should I? Do I even want to? Could this be the solution? Was orgasm better than meditation? Could I picture the journalist's face while I was coming? Would he be "the one," my healer, my sexual god?' Probably not but in respect of Beatrice's game and good intentions, I placed the dildo gently in my bag.

In exchange, I gave Beatrice a gift, my little traveling toy, what is known as a Pocket Rocket—a small, but powerful vibrator. I thought it was pretty fabulous and hoped Beatrice would too.

Dissatisfied after a few days of playing with the Green Giant, I returned it to Beatrice. I just couldn't get pleasure with it. Even picturing the writer's face distracted me. I wanted a woman. Plus I was missing my tiny powerhouse of a sex toy, the Pocket Rocket...and girls. On top of all my frustrations of being unable to meditate and find inner peace, I couldn't get any physical satisfaction either. I was frustrated on more than one level: spiritually and sexually.

In the midst of my dilemma, my teenage neighbor Assad came over to try and seduce me. To tempt me, Assad outright showed me his penis. It was huge and I couldn't help but stare but still...he was a kid, still in his teens. Assad was proud showing me his member, and rightly so—it was pretty impressive. Here he was, offering me the chance to get laid. Assad always desired me, he said, and described how he envisioned us on top of the apartment-building roof, having a wild ride under the stars. He said hopefully, "Maggie do you smoke? Because we can go up on the roof and, you know...try things there."

I politely rejected Assad's kind offer, promising to have sex with him when he was older. "How old are you, boy?" I asked.

"I'm old enough for you," he said. "I can prove it."

"Or do you need to prove something to yourself? "I wondered. "Because if it's 'yes,' I'm not the answer. You need to find someone younger." As I said this, I could see Assad visibly deflating. It was as if I'd punched him in the stomach. He walked out of my apartment with his head down and his pride wounded. 'Great, now I have to have to be guilty about breaking a boy's heart!' I thought.

I decided that one of my problems was having too much penis in my life. I found myself dreaming about the women I craved. I missed my Argentinean experience—even the extreme heat of the climate—and my time with the ladies.

My dream came true a month later. I was back at the JFK. This time, it wasn't to escape, but to pick up Rita at the airport. My Argentinean lover was coming to New York for a visit. We'd stayed in touch via Facebook and through other messenger Apps. I loved chit-chatting with Rita and keeping our flirting game going on the Internet. She helped me learn more Spanish while I taught her some of the most important English words. But the language barrier didn't matter when we were together, electronically, or in person.

When Rita got into my car, we exchanged a deep, passionate look, and we knew where we should head first. Destination: my house. The only problem was that Beatrice was already there with her new boyfriend. She'd left her boyfriend and moved into my place, causing my lovely husband to move out. It was too much for him to handle. Apollo decided to find a new temporary place and forge ahead with his own life. He had a problem dealing with the fact that I shared my attentions with others, and I totally understood that. Although I truly loved Apollo, I was looking for more. I hoped to find it in Rita.

Being with Rita in New York was like taking a trip back to Argentina. It was a shift of time and place when Rita and I took a ride together in my bed. I really enjoyed having her stay with me in New York although it wasn't exactly the same as it had been in Buenos Aires. Maybe because I wasn't on holiday and had to work. Plus the icy weather didn't help. At times, I felt confused by my emotions. Rita...Beatrice...Apollo...which one was my soul mate? Which would I ultimately end up with?

Jenny and her partner were back in New York too. The four of us celebrated Rita's arrival in the US. We were all at restaurant in downtown Manhattan when I realized how crazy the situation was. What the fuck I was doing there? At some point, we all were sharing same girl. Jenny's current love interest was the reason Jenny and I had officially ended our "friendship with benefits." Plus, when we'd met a few years ago at a wine tasting, Jenny's present girlfriend had stolen ex from me. It was a wild, crazy, lesbian square dance where we changed partners, stole partners, then found ourselves alone. It was all too much for me to handle, this mishmash of emotions. I was wondering how I could politely make a u-turn or back off the highway.

I didn't have to wait long for things to get resolved. The solution came all by itself. After using hand signals and sign language—and a little help from Goggle Translate—Rita and I tried to straighten things out between us. I told her that our relationship wasn't the same as it was in Argentina. Back there, we had a spontaneity which couldn't be transported anywhere else. In response, Rita wrote a good-bye letter to me with Jenny's help. At one point, I wasn't sure which one was talking to me, Jenny or Rita. I got the feeling they both put themselves into it and were trying to tell me something. Other times, it felt like Jenny was putting worlds into Rita's mouth. Blah, blah, blah…about the culture differences. Blah, blah, blah…about miscommunication. Blah, blah, blah about the different stages of life we were in. What bullshit!

With this ridiculous letter, I lost both Jenny and Rita, but also gained a new friend. Since Beatrice had moved in, we decided to stop fooling around, but now everything had changed. When we became roommates, we also realized that we were soulmates. We supported one another in difficult times and shared happiness during good times. Beatrice and I focused more on yoga and meditating, trying to find peace of mind. Spending time together was the best cure for our mutual broken hearts. We had good, clean fun and even spiced it up with a bit of wickedness. When we were doing laundry in our mutual ex's building (Arron and her ex boyfriend lived in the same apartment house, remember) by Prospect Park, we laughed out loud about how crazy it all was.

Everything seemed to be working out between my hubby Apollo and me, too. Although we were living apart, I was making progress in my married life with him. I was trying to be a good wife, even a long distance one. He and I were so different but I tried to focus on the similarities we shared. Apollo and I worked on improving our sex life. The Kama Sutra became our Bible. We had fun visiting each other, watching movies, having sex and sharing morning hugs.

As the days passed, my unpleasant New York wintertime was filled with love and wine. It seemed perfect...for a while. But since I'm easily bored and also gay, it soon felt dull and flat. Morning coffee and quiet time was all I thought I needed from Apollo. Plus a little sex thrown in for good measure. He seemed to understand this...or was it just me projecting my feelings on him? My sexual relationship with Apollo was just a dalliance, an amusing way to pass the time. But then I discovered that he had feelings for me. How stupid and careless I was to ignore it and pretended there was nothing more but great sex. Apollo was my husband with benefits, and that was all that mattered to me. But once again, it wasn't enough.

On Valentine's Day, Beatrice called, saying that she'd just met a nice, single, gay girl at Limbo, the bar where she worked. Beatrice wanted me to meet her. Right now. When I hesitated, she asked, "Maggie, what are you doing?"

"Nothing. I'll probably go early to bed," I told her. "I need some sleep."

"Hell no, you don't," Beatrice said. Not tonight. Just forgot everything that's been happening and get your ass over here."

"Since when have you become so aggressive?" I wondered. "Is this really you? What have you done with Beatrice?"

"Just get down here," she laughed.

"This better be good," I told her. I did a quick fix-up of my makeup then headed to the bar. Already bored with being a dutiful wife, I didn't even think twice. In less than an hour, I was at Limbo and ready for fun. A cute girl smiled at me when I walked in. Full of trust in Beatrice's taste, I wasn't disappointed. I liked what I saw right away, without even talking to her. I gave Eva one of my best smiles. We immediately clicked. My lovely friend Beatrice was right, as always. By now, she knew me—and my type—well. Eva was beautiful and adorable. A bit on the young side, but who cares on this once-a-year day for lovers. For most of the day, I'd almost forgotten that it was Valentine's Day but I was forced to remember with all of those foil hearts decorating the bar

Eva and I barely talked; we mostly kissed. "Mmmm...yummy...gosh" was all that came out of our mouths almost the whole time we were together that night. Eva and I kissed in Limbo then in another gay bar in Manhattan called Crazy Nanny's, where we decided to spend the rest of the night. (They had a popcorn machine with free popcorn, which was a nice perk.) The place was full of hot-looking girls. I couldn't stop staring at them, which I did while taking breaks from kissing my new treasure. Eva's mouth was so tasty that I was ready to take her home. I didn't though. Instead, we headed to another bar back in Brooklyn. Kissing all night long, we lost track of the time and ended up in my car, groping and smooching. I couldn't take Eva home because my lovely husband was probably there, waiting for me.

Drunk and tired but satisfied, when I got back home Apollo was already asleep. Beside him was a still-fresh and fully open red rose on my side of the bed. I guess he'd wanted to surprise me for Valentine's Day, which I'd spent with another woman, not him. I felt terrible. Even the memory of the sweet kisses I'd shared with Eva wore off. As quietly as I could, I crawled into bed next to my husband, and tried not to wake him up.

Chapter 9
Canada, Oh, Canada…and Hamsa

At least 40 students were taking same class but I noticed Hamsa immediately. Sitting in the middle of the classroom, she was absolutely my type with these big, deep, magnetic eyes that just drew me in. I had the feeling it would just be a matter of time before something happened between us. When I looked at Hamsa, it felt like the distance, the people between us, didn't exist at all. In the crowded lecture hall, it was only two of us, at least in my imagination. It I knew that Hamsa would be more than just a friend. A strange sensation, it went beyond attraction. Still involved with Arron at the time, I decided to fish a little bit more, to check Hamsa out, dig deeper, and yes, to pursue her.

It was no secret that I was bored with Arron. Many years had passed since we first met. The excitement, the newness of our liaison, was long gone. Our relationship had become more like a partnership: we woke up every day together, did things together and went back to bed together. It never varied. Our days were always the same and I was looking for something more. I was looking for "different." A young Muslim woman, Hamsa was definitely different. I was struck by her deep, soulful eyes.

Little did I know that Hamsa checking me out too. The next day, she moved closer to me in class. It was more than just simple curiosity. There was something in the air that I couldn't describe, a connection. But was there something else as well?

When Hamsa changed her seat, I was surprised, paralyzed, and couldn't say a word. I was only able to throw her a few shy smiles which she returned in response. Hamsa always had the ability to make me feel shy, and this rarely happened to me. I could count the times on my fingers when girls made my cheeks blush when I spoke to them. I didn't want it to be obvious and tried my best to hide it. I attempted to avoid looking in her direction but my eyes kept getting drawn to her. Besides, I was already in a relationship, albeit a bad one. I shouldn't be so drugged, so hypnotized by another woman. But damn, I was, and I couldn't help it. Did I want to help it? Probably not.

I didn't know anything about this black-eyed Turkish girl. Was she gay, bisexual or straight? Was she interested in me? Was I about to become her first girl? Was I her science experiment? I couldn't begin to guess but there was definitely something more in her eyes, something more than friendship. Time would tell. I was determined to get to know her. But how? I already had a girlfriend and I didn't have the time to pursue another. Looking back, I think it was the unexplained, the mystery of Hamsa that made me desire her more.

One day, in the middle of Manhattan, our paths crossed by chance. My heart leaped when I saw Hamsa but we only exchanged polite smiles and a pleasant hello. The same thing happened on a Brooklyn street, another haphazard meeting. But again, we didn't speak, just exchanged smiles, hellos, and moved on. That was it. The semester drew to a close and Hamsa went back to Turkey. That chapter in our lives ended abruptly. I never knew if she was into me like I was into her. And now I would probably never know.

About three years passed. I sometimes thought of Hamsa with a bit of sadness and regret. I felt like I'd missed my big opportunity with her and that our potential relationship was cut off without ever having started. Things were left so open-ended. But my intuition kept telling me that it wasn't over. How would it be possible to connect with Hamsa, though? I didn't have a phone number. I had no address. I didn't have a clue where she was or how I could reach out to her. Deep inside, I knew I should have made a move and beat myself up about not pursuing her when I had the chance. What harm would there have been in trying? I truly believed that people met for a reason. The situation with Hamsa made me promise myself that the next time I saw her, I would take a chance and go for it. Whatever "it" was.

I couldn't have been more surprised when Hamsa turned up. I just couldn't believe it...there was my dream girl, walking in front of me on campus. It was just two of us. Nobody else was around. It was right in the middle of a bridge that connected two buildings, a few days after Arron had broken up with me. Little did I know that Hamsa had just divorced her husband. I knew that our meeting on the connecting bridge was symbolic. I was convinced that Hamsa and I should both take a walk together, heading the same direction. We should give our budding relationship a chance and get to know each other better. We were both single, looking for opportunities and the adventure that comes with it. But she and I hadn't even talked to each other yet.

I couldn't mess it up this time and luckily, I didn't. I was able to construct a full sentence, instead of sputtering my usual tongue-tied hello before moving on. I cleared my throat and took a deep breath. "Is that you, Hamsa?" I said. "Do you remember me? We took a class together years ago."

Hamsa smiled in recognition and her dark eyes shone. "Yes, of course I remember you, Maggie." Then, "What are you doing here? I thought you graduated already."

"I did a year ago," I told her. "But I'm working on an event. The department knows I do catering and offered me a job."

"Nice. Congratulations!" Hamsa said.

There was a brief silence but I leapt right in. "What you doing here? I thought you left the US a long time ago. You were about to get married, right?"

"I'm back for a year or so, taking other classes here. And yes, I was married but so many things have happened since then..."

A little light bulb blinked on in my brain. Was she trying to tell me that she was gay? I seized the moment, determined to find out. "Do you want to meet and talk about it over a coffee or lunch?" I said quickly.

"That would be great!" Hamsa told me. "Give me your number and we'll plan something."

I found out that Hamsa was not only back in New York and back in school, but that she was working in a nearby restaurant. So, she'd already established roots here in Brooklyn. This gave me hope that my "second chance" with her might materialize into something and that we might take another step in our strange relationship which wasn't quite a friendship, wasn't quite a dalliance. Yet. What would be next, "friending" her on Facebook? Something more?

I didn't have to wait years to see Hamsa again. As seemed to be the norm with us, our encounter just happened spontaneously without planning. I wasn't too surprised when, after a nice walk with a friend in Coney Island, we decided to have a bite to eat at the first restaurant we saw. And guess who our server was? Hamsa. Our fateful meet-ups seemed normal. I told myself that if I just trusted in the universe, Hamsa would soon be my arms. And I was right. This was only the beginning, with the best yet to come.

Our lives were so busy that besides meeting on campus and at the restaurant where she worked, Hamsa and I didn't have the chance to go out for lunch or coffee as we had hoped. Then, one day, out of the blue, she called me on the telephone and asked if I'd be interested in going to Canada with her.

"Maggie, I know you travel a lot," she began hesitantly. "I'm about to take a tour to Canada next week. Do you want to come with me?"

I couldn't believe my good fortune. "Of course, I'd love to. I've never been there but I've always wanted to go. Who else is coming?"

"It's just two of us right now," she said. "But we can take another person if you have someone in mind."

I paused for a second, thinking that I wanted nothing more than to be alone with my beautiful Turk. "I'll ask around," I told her. "But I'm pretty sure it's too late. Most of my friends work or already have plans for the July 4th weekend."

"So, let's go together," Hamsa said. "We don't need anybody else. I'm so excited!" I could hear the enthusiasm in her voice, as she yelled out the last word. And just like that, we were heading to Canada.

I could still picture Hamsa and me sitting next to each other on the tour bus headed to Canada. Hamsa and I were the only non-Chinese people on the bus. As long as I was with Hamsa, nothing else mattered. I was happy the universe was finally giving me the chance to get to know her better. Not only was I visiting a new place but I was also discovering my new love. My patience had paid off. I looked forward to five days of getting closer to Hamsa. Especially after three long years of wondering if I'd ever see her again.

The minute I boarded the bus, I felt comfortable with Hamsa. From the start, we joked around and had serious political and religious discussions. Not only were our views and our senses of humor similar but it looked like we were both were batting for the same team. I was sure Hamsa was a bi-girl like me.

Instead of being drudgery, the time Hamsa and I spent on the bus was absolutely wonderful. Sitting side by side for hours, we had no choice but to get to know each other better. She was already aware of my sexual preferences—that I liked girls—but I still wasn't 100% certain about hers. Although Hamsa mentioned her marriage a couple of times, nothing more was said about it. But the way she looked and behaved were signs that she had already been with a woman. I'd had an intuition about this all along.

Now that she'd finally broken up with her husband, Hamsa asked me personal questions about my sex life. I was pretty sure she was hiding something about herself. I wondered if cultural taboos about same-sex relationships were preventing her from fully opening up to me. I knew that her religion considered homosexuality a big no-no. On that long bus ride, I worried that maybe I was asking Hamsa too many questions. But alone with her, I wanted her and nothing could stop me from pursuing her.

For the five days we spend together on the Canadian tour, nothing happened between us sexually but we grew closer emotionally. We reached the stage where we were not only traveling together, sharing time, places and experiences, but we were also sharing emotions.

When we visited the CN Tower in Toronto, an amazing thing happened which I'll never forget. At an elevation of 1,815 feet, the CN Tower was the world's tallest building and free-standing structure when it was completed in 1976. With a glass floor, the Tower is one of the biggest, scariest tourist attractions in the world. It's an incredibly weird feeling walking on the glass floor, with the view of the city literally under your feet. Your brain plays tricks on you and makes you feel like you're losing balance—and losing control.

For me, an adrenaline junkie, it was an incredible experience. Brave enough to overcome the odd feeling of walking on air, I tried to encourage my Turkish girl to do the same thing. One look at Hamsa and I could see that she was scared to death. Her normally beautiful olive complexion was white with fear. I took her hand and slowly pulled her closer to me as in the middle of the glass floor. Instead of resisting, Hamsa came toward me. She trusted me. I saw it in her eyes. She overcame her fear at my side. It was a wonderful feeling. Emotionally, I broke through to her. "Maggie," she began. "I always say I don't care if I live or die but right now, I feel like I don't want to die." I let Hamsa enjoy her new-found strength while I enjoyed the sensation of her hand in mine. I felt like I just conquered the world—and Hamsa.

After that bonding experience on the CN Tower, there were few other moments where Hamsa and I totally connected. One was simply having coffee together on the shores of Lake Ontario early in the morning. The beauty of nature surrounded us like a warm blanket. Temptation was there also. Both Hamsa and I sensed it but we ignored it. With the sun rising about the lake, I felt the sensation rising within us too, but neither Hamsa or I acted upon it. I don't know why. Fear of rejection? Fear of intimacy? Our trip to Canada was wonderful but it was over way too soon.

When the bus arrived in Chinatown and all of the other passengers got off, Hamsa and I stood in the middle of the crosswalk of East Broadway, clutching each other. Neither of us wanted to let go. Our lingering, last hugs defined everything I was waiting for. I hoped it was a sign of more to come.

Our next meeting was supposed to be a regular coffee date but it turned out to be a horror. Hamsa called me, suggesting we take a stroll with a cup of coffee on the High Line. I'd never been to the High Line, which is an abandoned elevated railway track on Manhattan's West Side, recently refurbished as a gorgeous walkway above the city and planted with beautiful greenery. It sounded like a great place for a coffee date, so I agreed immediately. I took the train to the city, looking forward to a good date with my Turkish dream girl.

As I walked toward the High Line, Hamsa suddenly jumped out in front of me. She'd been hanging out at the bar nearby, waiting for me. Not even noon, I thought it was a bit early to drink, and Hamsa already seemed tipsy. I tried to protest but she pulled me inside. I wasn't surprised that we were the only customers in the bar. This worried me because on our trip to Canada, Hamsa didn't drink. I discovered that she had an alcohol problem but she told me it was under control. Only now she was out of control, being drunk so early in the day. I had a feeling something had happened to spark her drinking. I took a deep breath and waited to see what would come next.

At the bar, Hamsa was falling all over me, saying that she tried to hide it but she had feelings for me from the very beginning. She also admitted that she first noticed me while she was wearing a hijab (a veil that covers a Muslim woman's head and chest). Obviously, when she was fully covered, I didn't recognize her. She just looked like a regular Muslim woman passing by on campus. But I'm surprised I wasn't struck by her beautiful eyes.

At the bar, Hamsa kept trying to kiss me. I still wanted her but not when she was this drunk. She asked if I could be her girlfriend. "Please be mine," Hamsa slurred. "Be my girl and only mine. Can you do it, please? Can you forget about the others?" Hamsa was so drunk that she was almost screaming. I hadn't done anything wrong. Who was she to talk to me like this and make a scene?

Shocked, I didn't know what to do and say. It was a nightmare. The dream girl I'd pined away for had turned into a drunken monster right before my eyes. When she'd had too much to drink, Hamsa turned from sweet to aggressive. How could this be happening? I'd fantasized so much about our first kiss, about being with Hamsa. I didn't want it to happen in a dark, smelly bar with her sloppy drunk.

The magic between Hamsa and me was gone in one moment. It put me into a foul mood. I couldn't do anything but take a taxi back home. Hamsa came along with me, saying that she didn't want to be alone. Instead of going to her own place, Hamsa insisted she come home with me.

As the door to my apartment closed, Hamsa was already on me. I didn't regret it though, even knowing, it was wrong. The night was long and tedious but I finally got what I'd wanted for last few years. Was I happy? Definitely not. I was disappointed and sad, if anything. Maybe the universe was sending me a message and for years, had been trying to protect me from what just happened. Or maybe it was my karma kicking me in the ass for being selfish and stubborn, willing to do anything, even the wrong thing, to get what I want.

Although I'd fed my desire to have Hamsa, I still wasn't satisfied. I wanted her sober. I wanted her to be fully aware of our lovemaking, not falling-down drunk. This is why I decided to give Hamsa a second chance. Everybody deserved at least that, I told myself. In retrospect, I was naïve to expect someone with a serious drinking problem to change their ways just like that.

My next encounter with Hamsa was at a Thanksgiving party at my place. I'd invited only a couple of my friends that year, Hamsa among them. I was excited to be cooking for people I cared about, Hamsa included. I was counting on having a better date (and sex!) with her than the last time. I believed our disastrous date that started at the High Line was an isolated incident and it wouldn't happen again. Our time together in Canada had been great but Hamsa had also been alcohol-free. Feeling optimistic, I tried to forget about our ill-fated first time and focus on the future.

Thanksgiving started out nicely, with food, games and dance. Time flew by and everybody seemed to enjoy the night. I was full of hope that this time with Hamsa would work out perfectly. But I wasn't prepared for what happened next. The party turned to be a disaster. Again, alcohol was to blame. Hamsa got so wasted that she wasn't able to communicate with rest of the world and worst of all, with me. She was so drunk, she couldn't even talk. I gave up on her and put her to sleep in my bed, disappointed again.

The door to my apartment opened and in walked my Polish beauty Beatrice with her new boyfriend James in tow. I hadn't seen Beatrice since Hurricane Sandy in August, but we were still dating, more or less. The night had brightened up a bit. Thrilled to see each other again, Beatrice and I hugged and kissed. It was a long, sweet kiss on the lips. Her new guy didn't seem to mind.

Feeling like I needed some air, I left Hamsa asleep on my bed and went out for a drink or two with Beatrice and James. I literally kicked out rest of my friends and ran away from my place. It was a relief not having to keep an eye on everything. I felt jailed in my own apartment instead of having fun at my party. Having a couple of drinks outside sounded perfect.

Beatrice, James and I took a ride to Park Slope in search for a good bar. We managed to find one still open. About four in the morning, Pacific Standard was full. Finally, I could get something to drink and forget about what had just happened with Hamsa. It felt good to be with Beatrice again, even with James there. She and I got cozy and kissed again. We turned the evening into a date, ignoring our new lovers…hers right next to us and mine sleeping off a drunk in my bed. Reluctantly, after Thanksgiving, I decided to cool things off with Hamsa.

Apollo and I had been planning a trip to Mexico together but he wasn't able to get the time off from work. Upset and angry at him, I considered inviting Hamsa to join me, then immediately thought better of it. I knew that taking a trip with her wasn't a good idea. Although our time in Canada was great, I now knew that three was a crowd: Hamsa, me and alcohol. Her drinking problem left no room for anything else. I'd already given her two chances and I was pretty sure a relationship with Hamsa wasn't going to work if she kept drinking.

I decided to go to Mexico alone.

Chapter 10
Mexico Lindo

There I was, in Cancun, without Apollo or even Hamsa. I had a lot of time alone to think and connect the dots, looking back over the last few months between Hamsa and me. The relationship I hoped would blossom hit a roadblock and it ended up with me having a broken heart. Again. Both my husband and my Hamsa had let me down. Life had been very intense recently so I tried to convince myself that maybe it was a good thing that I take a trip solo, to think.

I'd made too many wrong moves the past few years, to the point that everything seemed to grow and accumulate, threatening to bury me. I was constantly pursuing pleasure without looking at the consequences of my actions. I didn't understand that what I did affected others. My karma would reach me, I thought, and bite me in the ass. I could almost feel the sourness of it all, the bitter taste, while drinking from life's cup.

But I tried to enjoy my quiet time in Cancun, on the beautiful Yucatan peninsula. Nobody could take that away from me. I let the calm ocean breeze take my thoughts away. I grabbed a piña colada, downed it fast, and comfortably set my body on a beach chair. I let the sun take care of the rest, rebooting my body and soul with its energy and warmth. I was aching for some relaxation, beach time and the heat of the sun. I soon grew cheerful, slowly drifted away on a piña colada breeze, and fell asleep on the beach. But damn, I was dreaming of her! Hamsa... The things that had recently happened between us had followed me across the globe, refusing to let me forget them, even while I slept.

The way I saw it, I had two choices: either face my problems and solve them or hide myself from them. But I knew that hiding from them was impossible. They'd follow me wherever I went, like they had now, not even letting me fully enjoy my vacation. Or I could just let go of them by putting them down on paper. That would be my temporary relief until I headed back to New York and took care of things for good. I grabbed a pen and my journal and dug deep inside to the past. To Hamsa.

Yes, the universe shifted once again, and there I was, in Mexico, alone, dreaming of my dark-eyed Turkish beauty. I needed a break from driving headlong into the raging storm that was my life and to rethink my budding relationship with Hamsa. Writing in my journal, I vowed to analyze my choices, and hopefully, to make my decision with wisdom, not based on desires of the flesh. I tried to review my life honestly up to this point and silently promised to "fix" myself. This would be the first, most important step. Then I was sure everything else would fall into place.

But it had been almost a year since I started saying, "I must fix myself." Although it became my mantra, I spent a lot of time ignoring it. Each time I tried, something new happened to break my focus and I broke my promise to myself. Either it was a new girl teasing me or an old girlfriend coming back to haunt me or my endless quest for adventure. I could blame other people and other things as much as I wanted but deep down I knew the real problem was me. I was my own worst enemy.

I decided to take it one step at a time, and to make those steps tiny baby-steps. Counting my blessings, I was glad to be in beautiful Mexico alone without someone else to distract me. I dedicated my time to scuba diving, yoga and meditation. It was just me and the things that made me happy, nobody else to gunk it up. I was enveloped by the things that gave me peace my mind, far away from New York's crazy pace and people. In Mexico, I woke up early every morning to meditate and do yoga. Then I went scuba diving. It was a perfect existence.

Spending time underwater really relaxed me. Life beneath the sea seemed to be so organized, so well-defined. I loved escaping from the chaos that went on above the sea and clearing my mind underwater. I contemplated all I saw around me, from the vibrant coral, sea anemones and the aquatic life. I wondered if the turtles and parrotfish had lives as complicated as mine. I wanted to be part of this calm world as long as possible but my tank was getting empty pretty fast. I continued to be amazed by the calmness, simplicity and slow-motion life under the water's surface. Enjoying this spectacular underwater show for as long as I could, I slowly and reluctantly resurfaced.

It was time to move on. Merida, a beautiful colonial city which was inland, would be my home for the next few days. It was just as stunning as Cancun but in a different way. The biggest city on the Yucatan Peninsula, Merida is the Yucatan's capital with 60% of its population of Mayan ethnicity. I found the Mayan people to have proud, beautiful faces, like human sculptures, with pronounced cheekbones and strong lines. (And deep, dark eyes, just like my Hamsa!) Merida's architecture was just as impressive. Its culture was rich, with the influence of the British, French and Dutch prominent in it. Recently, because of the huge influx of Americans and Canadians, Merida had become a very popular bohemian-looking place. The streets were full of its gorgeous crafts: brightly woven clothing, hammocks and bracelets. I fell in love with the old part of the city with its charming, cozy restaurants and cafés, where life in Merida seemed to be centered.

I had family in Merida who invited me to stay with them. Otherwise, I never would have known about this gorgeous place. An easy three-hour bus ride from Cancun, it went almost from one edge of the Yucatan Peninsula to the other. Merida was exactly what I needed. I welcomed the escape to this colonial Mexican paradise. In addition to having mental and physical distance from New York, I also had my relatives for support. Who else can you count on when you're confused about life but family? I escaped to the safe and quiet zone of my cousin Adam's beach house. There, I could continue focusing on yoga and meditation, while being surrounded by people who asked nothing from me but my presence. I put my adventurous life and my quest for romance to the side for now. In exchange, I was surrounded by the beauty of nature and didn't count on anything happening other than trips to the beach, exercise and quiet moments inside my own head. I was mentally exhausted from my excitement overload in my private life and was thoroughly enjoying my brief but calm vacation in Mexico.

After few days of meditation I felt revived and reenergized. When the time came, I was ready to go back to civilization and take on everything that went with it. I'd already decided to resolve things with my Turkish girl when I got back to New York. But I still had a couple more days to enjoy Merida. I planned on exploring the town and getting lost in its charismatic streets and sampling the delicious foods in its native restaurants.

The huge hacienda where my cousin Adam lived was owned by a Canadian friend of his. Yves was throwing an open-house party for his friends, which coincided perfectly with my arrival. The hacienda soon filled with people, a nice mix of Americans and Canadians who were mostly artists either living in or visiting Merida. The wine and conversation flowed freely. Everyone was impressed by the French architecture and exquisite arrangement of the house. Both the furniture and the layout of the rooms were perfect. I grabbed a glass of a good wine and joined an informal tour of the house, visiting each corner and marveling in it.

A little overwhelmed and bit tipsy, I then joined the people crowded around a large table covered with local foods. Stealing a few bites here and there, I enjoyed the ambiance, enveloped by conversation in English, French and Spanish. The food was delicious, the talk simple and pleasurable, and the wine even better. The only thing that was missing was romance. But I reminded myself that I was taking a break from it—romance was the root of most of my problems.

Suddenly, the door opened and in drove a hot Mexican girl on a motorbike. Blonde and attractive, full of confidence, she rolled her scooter across the tiled floor to the kitchen hall. Her energy and smile left me speechless. The girl looked at me as she climbed off her bike and I met her gaze. Without words, we showed our interest in each other. In the blink of an eye, kinky Maggie was back. I'd forgotten all about my temporary vow of chastity.

Five minutes later, I was on the back of Melisa's scooter, my body glued to hers. Melisa was more than happy to give me a tour of Merida. Being good, religious girls, we stopped at an old church first. Taking pictures, we hugged and got closer and closer enough at the back of the church. It was the best, totally spontaneous date I'd ever had. Once again, the language barrier didn't matter. Our bodies, our emotions, took over, and the rest just came naturally.

Immediately, I felt good again. My dalliance with Melisa got me back on track, so to speak. The misbehaving Maggie I'd missed had returned. Sexually fulfilled and reborn, I was ready to go back to New York and face the music.

Chapter 11
Back in the New York Groove

Back in New York, I needed to have a heart-to-heart talk with my Turkish friend—about her drinking problem and our relationship. Hamsa knew that I'd gone to Mexico on my own without even saying a word to her. She should have been there with me on the plane, beside me scuba-diving, on the beach next to me...and in my bed. But her problems with alcohol prevented us from moving forward into the deeply loving relationship I was sure we were capable of.

As soon as I returned from Mexico, it was back to reality. It seemed to be one battle after another. First, I was fighting with a mailbox stuffed full of letters. It was packed so tight, I couldn't get anything out. During my short absence, it didn't look like anyone had emptied it. I wondered how the letter carrier was able to shove so many papers in such a small box. But, if they got in, they should be able to get out, right? Wrong.

I finally approached my mailbox like a puzzle game. (Kind of like I approached my life lately!) I started with the smallest letter that was rolled up inside of the others. One by one, I managed to extract my mail. The first letter I looked at wasn't even for me. It was for my ex, Arron. Frustrated, I reached out for another, a bit bigger in shape and easier to get at. Grrr... that one had my husband's name on it. Feeling forgotten by the whole world, I pulled out another in hopes that it was for me. What the hell? It was my mailbox and there were no letters for me in it at all. There was even an envelope for Beatrice, who'd moved in a couple of months ago.

Angry at the universe, I shut the mailbox and refused to open it again for another week. This was my apartment, my life, and it looked like I didn't belong there at all. There were too many people in it that was the problem. But where did I fit into this mess? I decided to finally organize my "box," and my life.

On my agenda for the next few weeks was running, reading, writing and riding my motorcycle. I was fully enjoying my new lifestyle as an evolved Brooklyn woman. I was more passive than active in terms of my relationships with people. Away from everyone, Prospect Park became my second home and sanctuary. I spent hours running along its tranquil paths, and nestled in its hills, writing. Prospect Park became my new love, my quiet zone. I needed its comforting acres to get lost in, to think, to reevaluate my life.

Spring came, then spring turned into summer. The days passed quickly, melting one into the other with no drama whatsoever. Brooklyn looks best in the springtime, I think, with the bright yellow forsythia and pink cherry blossom trees all around. But summer is a close second with the roses in everyone's front gardens competing for attention and the gentle sunshine. All was good and quiet on Planet Maggie.

At the end of June, the streets of Manhattan turned into a wave of colorful rainbow flags and posters that announce Gay Pride Day. The entire city seems to celebrate. Taking a break from my mellow lifestyle of books and nature, I decided to give some support and participate. I figured it would be a good opportunity for me to slip back to into the New York groove.

My partners in crime were Mary, my Sugar Mama, my best friend Beatrice and my friend Gia. We took great pleasure in watching the lively floorshow which is Gay Pride in New York, including some scandals and drama. It was better than a TV show because this was live and this was real. But it was also incredibly crowded. Getting from one place to another was literary impossible. It took us hours to get from midtown to Greenwich Village, which was only a couple of miles. Gia and I were supposed to meet up with friends but thousands of other people were in the way. Crowds were gathering to watch the Gay Pride Parade.

We had to wait to cross the streets, blocked by police directing traffic everywhere we turned. We often stopped after few blocks to watch the parade while waiting for the crosswalk to open again so people could make their way to the other side of the street. Every few minutes, when there was a break in the parade, the police let pedestrians cross. As much fun as Gay Pride was, it was annoying for us fast-paced New Yorkers to be reduced to moving at a crawl.

One of these stops took us even longer than usual. The reason? A beautiful Moroccan-American girl who acted as though she owned the street. Loud and provocative, she smoked and drank with no fear of been ticketed, standing right next to an NYPD officer. I happened to be next to her, trying to watch the parade while waiting for the crosswalk to open again. She blew a cloud of cigarette smoke into my face and flashed me a bit of her cocky attitude. I turned to her angrily. "Can you please stop blowing the smoke in my face?" I asked, then tagging on for good pleasure, "Fuck you very much!"

Instead of getting angry, she looked at me with her innocent, childlike eyes and apologized. "I'm sorry," she said. "Let me buy you a drink."

Still mad, I refused her offer, thinking, 'Is she fucking crazy?' Yes, I think she was. I told her, "Oh, no thank you. I don't think it's a good idea. It looks like you already had enough to drink already."

Instead of leaving it at that, the girl just smiled and without a word, grabbed my hand and pulled me into bar. Before I knew it, I found myself standing there with strangers, doing shots one after the other. 'What a beautiful life this is,' I thought.

The Moroccan girl, whose name turned out to be Aisha, jumped over the bar. Without hesitation, she pushed the bartender away, and started pouring drinks for me and her friends. Feeling young, wild and drunk, we started fooling around, kissing and touching each other. Hey, it was Gay Pride Day, after all. The more we drank, the more we played.

Without even asking, Aisha pulled a makeup kit out of her bag and started working on my face. I don't know how or why she came up with the idea, but I didn't question it. I just enjoyed the touch of her soft hands all over my face, like little butterflies. Even intoxicated, I could tell that I looked nightmarish, like a clown, but it didn't matter. It was all good.

I couldn't resist Aisha being so close to me so I started kissing and biting her hands. She seemed to like it, even when it got more intense. Aisha and I were kissing each other's mouths now and in between kisses, she still tried to paint my face. What a beautiful time it was. But I wasn't the only one who Aisha kissed. She ran over to another table where she started kissing someone else. Aisha wanting to kiss with the whole world didn't bother me. For the past year, I tried not to let jealousy get into the way. I just wanted to enjoy the ride.

And enjoy, Aisha and I did. We ended up right next to the kitchen, fooling around. Terrified, the kitchen staff, moved dishes away from us as we teased and kissed and groped and rolled around on the counters and tabletops. It was a Gay Pride Day to remember. Even though I never saw Aisha again.

That summer was full of memorable experiences. Another that stands out in my mind was when my Chinese friend...I'll call her 'Jasmine"...took a spur-of-the-moment trip. Anything with Jasmine was always a wild, crazy adventure. I lusted after her from the first we met many years before. At my wedding dinner, I had fantasies of fondling and fingering her under the table. (I know, I'm terrible!)

The year before, Jasmine jumped on my tour bus before it left for Washington, DC. Although surrounded by 30 people, we cuddled not only on the bus, but spent most of that trip in bed. I didn't even hide our romance from the people on the tour. Jasmine and I danced and drank at a bar near our hotel, letting the sexual energy between us build. It finally led us into bed together, something I'd wanted for many years. So, when Jasmine invited me on a day trip, I couldn't refuse, even though I knew I was playing with fire. Again.

The phone rang early one Saturday morning, and there was Jasmine's sexy voice, tempting me. "Maggie honey, lets go to Hamptons for a day."

"The Hamptons? What for?" I'd spent a summer in the Hamptons with Arron and now had completely wiped it from my memory. Our time in the Hamptons was far from being a pleasure trip for Arron and me—we both worked our butts off there. New to New York then, I did whatever "sitting job" I could: babysitting, dogsitting, dogwalking, housesitting, while Arron was a nanny for a rich family. I was grateful when Arron asked her boss to hire me on as help in their Hamptons house for the summer. Although I didn't like the job, I knew it was just temporary, a way of making money, so I stuck with it. I appreciated the generous pay, the time I got to spend with my girlfriend, and all above, the Hampton's beach and town.

While I space out with my Hamptons memories, I totally forgot Jasmine was on the other end of the phone. She was still talking, explaining to me how we would get there and what she had planned for the day. "We can have dinner in the house and stay on the beach. My friend will drive us out there," Jasmine was bubbling.

I wondered if Jasmine's friend would stay with us or if we'd be alone. I hoped it was the last one. "Are you serious?" I asked. "Is he in love with you or what? Who is this guy?"

"He's just a friend. I'm taking my kids too because I want to show them the house and place," she explained. So now there was a guy and two kids thrown into the mix. Jasmine was getting impatient with me. "Are you coming with us? Please, Maggie, please..." She filled up the silence with more promises. "You and I could spend some time together. I don't care about the guy. He knows about you and me."

'Great,' I thought. I told her, "And he's probably counting on something to happen. A threesome, right?"

Jasmine laughed. "I don't care what he thinks or wants. Do you?"

"Hell, yes, I do," I told her. "But it's okay. Let's go, girl!" And away we went.

Jasmine knew where the house keys were hidden so we had easy access to the place. She'd worked for the family, taking over my dog-walking and house-helper job. Soon after Jasmine arrived in the US, we met at an event since we were both part of the catering staff. Like most New Yorkers, I multitasked and worked odd jobs to get by. Jasmine was so lovely that she caught my eye. I was attracted to her since then. I was thrilled when we finally consummated our lust on that Washington, DC trip. But before then, I couldn't stop thinking about her and looked for any occasion to see her and get to know her better.

Jasmine gladly took part in my little flirt games, enjoying the ride. After a while she broke up with her boyfriend and began dating my friend Mark, from work. To be honest, I knew I should have backed off at that point but I desired Jasmine so much that I didn't care. Throwing Mark into the mix made it even more intense. Seeing it as more of a challenge, I was hitting on Jasmine more and more. I didn't care that we all worked together or that we were all friends. I took Jasmine out to gay bars, Pride events or just to lunch or coffee. I tried to entertain Jasmine as much as possible, slowly introducing her to the gay world. I know I should have stopped seeing her, but I enjoyed the game too much.

It wasn't long before Mark and Jasmine married. I knew he was deeply in love with her, but even marriage didn't stop me from reaching my goal—having sex with Jasmine. I was pushing myself into her life more and more. I even helped her find a temporary job, trying to get closer to her in any way possible.

Besides my desire for Jasmine, there was a great connection between us. We understood each other. We got each other. We enjoyed spending time together and the romantic moments we shared. I liked looking at her slender body in the candlelight when we had dinner in a romantic restaurant. I liked watching her play with her long, straight, black hair when she talked to me. I liked her fresh, flowery perfume's smell when she leaned on me in a crowded gay bar. Jasmine had a very delicate, feminine face. She could look like a child one moment, then had toughness in her eyes the next. She was intriguing, intoxicating. I loved the prospect of spending time with her—even with another guy and her kids in the picture.

I hadn't been in the Hamptons for years and was looking forward to returning to the same house that was full of happy memories of Arron. We'd worked there three summers. I was grateful that the family took me on too, knowing that Arron and I were a couple. I think the host was secretly excited to have two lesbian lovers in his employ; the wife too. Yes, it would be nice to go back to the place that held such fond memories for me.

But returning to the Hamptons with Jasmine, her two teen-aged kids and her male "friend" Kris was a completely different story. Maybe Kris wasn't her lover but Jasmine had definitely seduced him enough to drive us more than two hours there. I didn't care who came with us, though—I just wanted Jasmine, no matter what. The only one who was left behind in New York was her husband Mark, who probably felt abandoned. But that wasn't my concern.

There I was, back on the Hamptons beach, enjoying every minute of it. The magnificent house faced the ocean, where I watched the sunset, alone. It was so beautiful that I broke into tears. The memories of good times hit me hard. I pictured Arron and me, everywhere I went: playing with the dogs, cooking meals together, like a happy family. All of that was gone now. I was alone, yet I had so many lovers. But did anyone love me like Arron had? And would anyone love me like that again?

Did I miss it? Did I miss the past and the time Arron and I had spent there together, closer than sisters? No. I think I was crying because I had a great time and now it was gone. Maybe I was mourning the past. Was I so cold and empty inside or did I just close the door on everything that had happened, trapping my feelings behind it? Maybe there was something wrong with me. Had I turned into an emotionless bitch? These thoughts ran through my head while tears ran down my cheeks.

I was also crying over the things I had done to myself after Arron and I broke up. I was aware of my bad behavior and the time I wasted on meaningless flirtation and sex games, but I was powerless to stop it. Was I a sex addict like some people had no control over sugar or alcohol—like my Hamsa?

I sobbed long and deep and hard. Maybe I'd ignored my emotions for too long and held them inside for too many years. They were only just now coming to the surface. Instead of holding back, I let the tears flow, and it felt good. I needed to cry. I needed the release. But I wasn't ready to change yet.

Watching the sun sink below the ocean, I shook off the tears and went back to the house. It smelled fantastic. Dinner was ready and the smell of cooked crabs filled the room. Jasmine had put on romantic music on and was serving our meal, wearing nothing but a bikini and a smile. "Where have you been for so long?" she wondered. "Did you get nostalgic?"

"Yes, sort of," I admitted.

"I noticed. That's why I left you alone, so you could be with yourself and the past," Jasmine added softly. "But now you're back with us. I have something delicious for you. You should taste it."

Was Jasmine talking about dinner or sex? Or both? The aroma of fresh seafood mixed with the desire in the air. It shook me out of my sadness. "I would love to taste it," was my response.

After we ate Jasmine's wonderful meal, I pulled on her hand and she got up to dance with me. The wine, the food, the music, had gotten the best of me. Afterwards, I got myself another glass of wine. Taking a deep breath, I sat on a bar stool and relaxed. Jasmine stood closer to me and said, "Let me in if you want to try it." Seconds later, she was on my lap, moving her hips up and down to the rhythm of the music, giving me my own private lap dance. I was already wet and I suspect she was too. I had another glass of wine, and another, getting lost in the line that blurred fantasy and reality.

We were being watched. By Kris (and Jasmine's children!) Our tipsy lap dance led to laughing and touching. The atmosphere became little too intense for all three of them. For more privacy, Jasmine and I took a walk on the beach, hoping it would help us sober up. But the strong ocean breeze didn't even help. If anything, it increased our desire. Still drunk, Jasmine rolled around in the sand like kids, except we kissed and groped each other. People strolling the beach began staring. Would one of them put two and two together and suspect that we were horny trespassers, staying in their neighbor's home without their permission? Both lost in a bittersweet moment, Jasmine and I ached for more, and soon. Even the fear of being arrested for trespassing didn't stop me from pushing further. My quest for pleasure was even bigger than my fear. The risk of being recognized as trespassers elevated my craving for more.

But Jasmine and I were thrown back into reality when we saw her son, who was about eleven years old, approaching us. Jasmine and I were still clutched together, covered in the sand. "Mom, you look cool," he said.

Jasmine just smiled and replied, "Okay, let's all run back to the house. It's getting dark."

"Great idea," I said, beside myself with desire. "Let's see who's faster." He ran and we followed, still a little drunk. Jasmine and I walked back, crookedly, leaning on each other's bodies.

Still slightly drunk and horny, Jasmine and I didn't want to stop the fun. When we were left alone again, we played around in an outside shower. Satiated for now, we went to bed. It was exactly same bed I used to sleep in with Arron years before. Sometimes life was so bittersweet.

After we got home from our dalliance in the Hamptons, things between Jasmine and me changed completely. When I called to check on her, she didn't pick up the phone. Feeling ignored, I tried again but there was no response this time either. No texts, not even a Facebook message. This was bizarre because Jasmine and I communicated all the time, sending silly texts and calling each other just to say hi. Sad and angry at the same time, I just gave up. I tried my best to forget Jasmine and our steamy night in the Hamptons.

Time passed. I was already focusing on new people and new adventures. Suddenly, from out of nowhere, Jasmine got in touch with me. At first I was angry. It took her more than two weeks to finally respond to my phone calls, and it was just one short text. But her excuse was so hard-hitting I had to forgive her:

> "Maggie, we can't meet anymore. My husband forbade me to see you and is threatening to send me and my kids back to China."

So that was it. But why didn't she tell me that right after the Hamptons trip instead of pulling a disappearing act? Mark was making Jasmine choose between me and her staying in the States. It was a difficult choice for her but I understood it completely. But once again, I was ditched. It was over.
The last words I texted to Jasmine were:

> "Why didn't you say so? You know that your status is more important to me and I wouldn't let such a thing happen."

But there was response from Jasmine at all.
Since I'd already lost one friendship, I didn't want to lose another. I decided to resolve my conflict with Hamsa, just as I'd promised to do after my Mexico trip. I wondered if I should try and find her to see if she was all right. On one hand, I was curious about how she was and hoped she had gotten her alcohol problem under control. On the other, I was disappointed that it hadn't worked out between us as I'd hoped. As curious as I was, I was afraid to get back together with Hamsa. I did miss her, even with all the bad things that had happened between us. But I still felt a strange connection to her. In the back of my mind, I was waiting to hear from her. It had been almost six months since that failed Thanksgiving dinner.
With Jasmine out of my life, Hamsa was constantly on my mind. I decided to make the first move and text her, just to ask how she was doing.
Hamsa replied immediately, saying that she'd been thinking of me non-stop as well:

"I was afraid to text you first and was hoping you would do it sooner or later. Thank you for getting back to me."

Then:

"Can I call you now so we can talk?"

Moments after my reply of, "Yeah, sure," my cell phone vibrated. For a second, I froze. I had my doubts. Should I pick up? Should I start everything with Hamsa all over again?

Of course, I picked up.

The first words out of Hamsa's pretty mouth were an apology. "I'm sorry for what happened," she said. "I understand why you didn't want to stay in touch with me."

I told her, "It shouldn't have happened this way. I hope you're okay now and that you feel better so we can hang out again." I did hope Hamsa realized she had a drinking problem and that she'd made an effort to change it during the almost half a year we'd been apart.

"All is good now!" she told me. "I'm back in New York from Turkey where I fixed it. Please, let's meet and talk again. I would love to see you, Maggie." I hesitated, thinking it over. Then Hamsa added softly, "Maggie, I'm really sorry for what happened and I'm so glad you got back to me." It all sounded so promising that I believed her. Still feeling connected and hoping she got a handle on her drinking, I gave Hamsa her third and final chance. How could I not?

It was Hamsa's graduation day and she invited me to be there. I came with Dina, a friend of ours. Having Dina as a buffer gave me more confidence. I truly believed that Hamsa was trying to work on her alcohol problem, but based on previous experience, knew she was unpredictable. Anything could happen with Hamsa…and it usually did.

I wasn't surprised when Hamsa introduced me to her professor, who also happened to be her lover. With curiosity in his smile, he said, "So, you're THE Maggie? Her girl?"

"Well, if she said so, then I guess I am. I'm definitely a friend. A close friend," I told him. Just to seem interested in him, I tagged on, "And I guess you're the one she's talking about at all time?" The Professor puffed up like a proud rooster when he heard that. It was an uncomfortable situation that I knew Hamsa had created for the sole purpose of making us feel awkward.

The Professor said, "Yes, it's me."

I nodded and responded, "Good," refusing to give Hamsa the satisfaction of seeing a confrontation and cutting off her little game at the knees. She looked a little disappointed that no one was fighting over her but quickly got over it.

It's true, I knew about the Professor, but had never met him in person. Besides working as a tour guide during the past few years, I also taught in a local college. The Professor and I both worked at the same school but in different departments. So, in addition to working at the same college, the Professor and I were also sharing the same girl.

I blamed the Professor as the reason everything had gone in a different direction than it should have with me and my Turkish ladylove. (Next to her alcohol problem, of course.) Why did she fall for him? Much older than Hamsa, was he a father figure? Maybe it was because all he asked of her was the pleasure of being with her. Whereas I asked for so much more: her heart, her devotion, her sobriety.

The Professor knew about me because Hamsa talked about us constantly. She'd told me this much. Hamsa couldn't choose between me and him and confessed to having feelings for both of us. She'd mentioned him to me occasionally. In the beginning of our relationship, it irritated me but when our relationship had hit a stumbling block, I didn't care anymore. The Professor became another one of Hamsa's quirks, one of her games. Since I was terrified of any real commitment, he was a safety net for me—his existence prevented me from getting too close to Hamsa. And isn't that what I really wanted?

But this dualism wasn't really working out well for Hamsa. Having different types of love for both the Professor and me, giving us each a part of her beautiful heart, was taking its toll on her. But with my already-complex life, this was the best possible arrangement we could have. It meant that I was free and unobligated to have any serious commitment with Hamsa. And it was an excuse to start "dating" again.

Alcohol is a great buffer. I found it was a perfect way for me to bury my true feelings. Pushing aside any questions that I might have a drinking problem myself, I realized that I always got into trouble when Hamsa and I were together. It wasn't hard to see that our relationship was going nowhere again but alcohol helped me cover up my worries. But after a while, I couldn't deny that Hamsa's plan to have both me and the Professor wasn't working out well. Basically, it was bullshit. But I still wanted her. I couldn't stop seeing her. What was the mysterious pull Hamsa had on me? The sex hadn't been great because she was usually sloppy drunk. I still don't know what drew me to her. All I could say is something in me still wasn't satisfied and I was determined to take our relationship to the bitter end until I found out.

Hamsa and I met at a motel near by my place. When I got there, I could feel that the bed was still warm. The cover and pillows were strewn across the bed. Was she taking a nap in the middle of a day? Was she drunk again? No, it meant that The Professor had just left. They had been making love there before she called me to come over. But I was emotionless. I felt nothing. It didn't bother me that he was with her few minutes before, fucking her in the same bed. I just wanted to be with her and maybe have sex with her. Was this just another of my erotic adventures? Was this just another way to punish myself?

I knew I was better than him and that I could give Hamsa what he couldn't. She had told me this much herself. Hamsa claimed that I could pleasure her like no one else. I felt ready for everything in this wonderful game where pain and pleasure were so closely knit together. The pain of wanting Hamsa and not getting her. The ache of "almost" but not quite. All I sought was that moment and the promise of pleasure that would come with it.

Apollo was very understanding when it came to me and Hamsa. Whenever I brought her home, he slept in the living room. On the nights he came home and found two beautiful girls in his bed, he curled up on the sofa with no problem. I knew Apollo was a true gentleman. Also, shy as he was, he wouldn't approach Hamsa and me sexually. I also knew that finally his dream came true: having two girls in his bed. Even if Apollo didn't participate, I think that's every guy's dream. What guy wouldn't like to have two girls in his bed? But he quietly stayed in the living room and never interrupted us.

I think the situation was already too much for Apollo to handle. Especially when Hamsa walked around the apartment totally naked. He didn't know what to do or what to say. His eyes wide with surprise, it seemed as if he couldn't believe what was happening. Even I was paralyzed when my nude Turkish girl stood in front of Apollo, talking to him with no embarrassment. He just stood there in the kitchen, trying to find different things to stare at. The refrigerator, the toaster... I can still see Hamsa now, her right breast jumping up and down while she squeezed and shook the honey from the bottle into our tea. She looked like Eve in the Garden of Eden, having a casual conversation with my hubby. Poor Apollo, he was so beside himself that he ended up with burned hands and spilled tea but I don't think he minded.

Hamsa even invited Apollo to join us in bed. But that nirvana moment didn't last long because when Hamsa realized how close sexually Apollo and I were, she kicked him out. I think she became jealous of our intimacy. The bed was too small for the three us, literally and figuratively. Although we enjoyed the aborted three-way and were ready for more, Hamsa wouldn't hear of it.

No matter how much I had of her, it still wasn't enough. I always wanted more. I also believed that after not seeing each other for six months, everything would change, but nothing had. I still saw the third party in our relationship as alcohol, not her professor lover. As far as I could tell, her drinking problem was gone. The Professor worried me less than alcohol did. I thought half a year was enough time to fix her drinking problem but I learned that it wasn't the case. It turned out to be just an illusion, a blind hope.

But Hamsa wasn't my only problem. Around the time she and I rekindled, I found myself in criminal court among a hundred other people. I almost got arrested. But thanks to my Polish savior, Beatrice, I only got a ticket. My crime? Littering, believe it or not. Besides the ticket, I had a court appearance. It could have been worse but because Beatrice was with me in the car, she saw everything and acted as my witness when the police ticketed me.

It happened after I attended my friend Gia's birthday party with Hamsa. The party was at the Wythe Hotel in Williamsburg which has a breathtaking view of Manhattan. We were running late so by the time Hamsa and I arrived, everyone already had few glasses of their favorite beverage and were having fun. The party was in full swing. I was sipping my drink slowly but it seemed like Hamsa was trying to make up for lost time. My intuition told me that this wasn't a good thing, the beginning of the end, maybe. We were there a few hours, which was more than enough for me. I wasn't feeling well and had this strange feeling that something bad was about to happen. I had a tough time convincing Hamsa to leave the party with me and go home.

When we left Williamsburg, Hamsa was acting strange. While I tried to drive, she was singing, yelling and pulling my shoulders. I tried to stop her but nothing worked. It only got worse, so bad, in fact, that I almost left her out on the street. In retrospect, I should have done that in the first place.

Hamsa asked me to stop for cigarettes, promising not to buy beer. "Remember, no alcohol!" I warned her as she left the car. I didn't want it in my car or in my home, where we were headed. But Hamsa ignored me, bought a bottle of beer and opened it. We began fighting. I threatened to leave her outside on the street. I didn't really care how far away it was from her place. I told her to throw her beer into a nearby trash can. Again, she refused. Angry, I grabbed the open bottle and threw it, missing the nearby garbage can I'd been aiming for.

This all happened while I was parked in a busy bus stop. Unfortunately, I didn't notice a police car parked there too. The next thing I knew, a light was shining in my eyes and a cop was at the side of the car. Hamsa had spilled her beer in my car and the whole thing reeked of alcohol. This didn't help the situation. To make matters worse, Hamsa told them that I had been drinking and driving. It was all a total lie. Why had my girl set me up like that? I was terrified that I'd get a DWI even though I was sober. I was dumbfounded. I didn't know what to say or do. Thank God Beatrice, who was sitting in the back seat, calmly explained what had really transpired. Believing her account of the incident, the police let me go with a ticket and a warning.

Strike three, Hamsa was out. I left my beautiful Turkish girl behind without looking back.

Chapter 12
North to Alaska

It would have been much healthier for me to focus on running, reading and writing as I had for the past few months before I'd rekindled with Hamsa. But instead, I did the worst thing I could possibly do: I fucked my brains out. Sex to me was like alcohol was to Hamsa. Was I a sex addict? Was I a whore? I didn't care. It felt good, so I did it.

But I had so much sex that it was like I had a sign on my back that said, "Fuck me." During that time, I had too many lovers to keep track of, too many choices, and I took advantage of them all. In the long run, I knew I wasn't going anywhere but I didn't care. I was tired of everything—the girls, the game-playing, the bars. I left my job and took the rest of the summer off to think. What better place than to escape than to Alaska? I really needed a change, needed to leave people and problems behind. I had an urge to be deep in nature, and going "into the wild" seemed like the best medicine I could take.

I really should have gone to Alaska with my lovely husband Apollo, who I still had a great time with and strong feelings for. But once again, he couldn't get away from work. Instead, I enticed my dear friend Durga to go with me. Durga was vegan, socially-aware, responsible and down-to-earth. A former Israeli officer, Durga's an activist as well. Unbelievably grounded, I knew she would be the best company for a trip like this. I hoped her calmness and levelheadedness would rub off on me.

Durga and I set off on our Alaskan cruise in late September. With my sophisticated yet earthy friend by my side, I hoped to do a lot of soul-searching on this trip and figure out what I really wanted in life, where I belonged, how I fit into the great scheme of things. Once again, my thoughts drifted back to my past. But instead of being nostalgic, with Durga's help, I was able to consciously make decisions and plan my future. Almost a year before, I had opened Pandora's box and now it was time to close it before it was too late.

Determined, I resolved to fix everything in my life, starting with social media. I cleared my Facebook page of "friends" who would hurt rather than help my evolution. I also cleared my phone of old texts I might look upon wistfully. I was starting with a clean slate. But there was one text that I always stopped on. It was from Lola. I couldn't delete Lola from my life, not yet. It wasn't over and honestly, it had just barely begun. Although things with Lola were still platonic, there was the promise of more. Always the promise of more. We'd flirted enough. I'd fantasized about her enough—even during Hurricane Sandy. I was tired of wondering where her mysterious tattoos were located, and wanted to take our relationship to the next level.

The day I was leaving for Alaska, I went for a run and ended up at Lola's office. It was a hot, late summer day. I was sweating and smelly but felt like nothing could stop me. My desire was bigger than anything else. I closed the door behind me and looked deeply and hungrily Lola's eyes. In them, I found surprise and a little panic for what might come next. I also detected desire. Lola knew I wanted something more; so did she. I closed her office door behind me.

The night before, Lola had emailed me a "confession letter" where she admitted how interesting she found me and how much she wanted me. I didn't know how to respond and knew she was waiting to hear from me. Instead, I just showed up. By doing so, Lola knew my response—that I wanted her too. Tired of this beautiful chasing game, I wanted more than just the hunt. I wanted her.

With the office door closed, I sat at Lola's desk and moved her chair closer to the computer. I began typing what I wanted to say: the truth. Finally, I learned the value in telling people what I really felt. Before now, I wasn't honest with people—or with myself. I felt a strange sense of calm as I sat at Lola's desk and typed. My words appeared on the computer screen:

1. "My life is already complex enough."
2. "And I'm trying to fix it."
3. "I'm the one who takes more risks, in this case."
4. "It's not healthy at all."
5. "Hmmm…"
6. "But I don't give a fuck."
7. "I already have a big mess."
8. "Please don't hurt me."

9. "And, I don't care what's going to happen next between us..."

Lola just typed back:

"I want more."

While I was typing, Lola was nervously moving around the room and talking a lot. The situation was obviously uncomfortable for her but at the same time, stimulating. Lola was speechless. The tension in the room was an incredible aphrodisiac for me. Her full breasts and nicely curved, full body were so close that I could feel her breath on my neck. Lola's short skirt exposed her lovely legs and her sweet perfume played with my senses. I smelled her, I felt her, I saw her. I so much wanted to taste and feel her. I was ready to jump right in and take her. My adrenaline level was high after my run and standing there beside Lola, I began to feel lightheaded. I leaned forward and kissed her.

My first kiss with Lola was light and feathery. Sweet. I craved more but stepped back. Even with her office door shut, anyone could walk in. I hadn't locked the door and didn't want to risk being discovered by Lola's coworkers.

But still, I asked myself, 'Why the hell did I stop?'

That question was still on my lips as Durga and I boarded the airplane to Vancouver where we'd catch our cruise ship to Alaska. Once we were in our seats, I could drift away and pass the long 10-hour flight inside my own head. Durga was very understanding and very undemanding. That's one of the things I liked about her as a friend. She didn't need to talk to me 24-7 and was happy to leave me with my own thoughts. And after all, we'd be spending weeks together on a cruise ship so we'd have plenty of each other's company. While Durga vegged out in the seat beside me, my thoughts turned to the lovely Lola.

A woman of many talents, Lola had tried her hand at crafting erotic stories, and they were wonderful. Well-written and full of delicious sexual details, the lesbian encounters were particularly intense. Was Lola teasing me? Was she sending me a silent message through them? Whatever was on Lola's mind, she had captivated me—with her dirty writing and with her enchanting eyes.

I was vaguely aware of Durga trying to interact with me in the seat beside me. After a few of my "Huhs?" Durga smiled and gave up. She knew I was in a different world. In my mind, I was still in Lola's office as I had been a few hours earlier. I kept picturing—and feeling—our stolen kiss during the whole flight to Vancouver. It was quick kiss but it was poignant, one that promised of more to come. I wanted more of everything about Lola: her sensual stories, her graceful body and her soul. I was hungry to learn more about her. Lola had nicely, quietly seduced me, put her spell on me. There was so much I wanted to discover. I dreamed of meeting her in a different place and time, so we could continue what we'd started in her office.

Lola's and my flirtation had been put on "pause" a few months before. After my orgasmic masturbation session with Lola during Hurricane Sandy we didn't run into each other very often. Too busy fooling around with other women, I almost forgot about her. Lola and I saw each other at work—meetings, holidays gatherings and other functions. I was always happy to see her, and vice versa, but I already had too much on my plate. Between Hamsa, Beatrice, Apollo and all the rest, my plate was overflowing! In the back of my mind, I knew my flirtation with Lola would start back up sooner or later. Although I was busy resolving my multiple lovers issues, I was still interested in her. I was just patiently waiting for the right time to come.

Lola's and my dalliance came back to life with the first signs of spring that next year, in 2013. From the beginning, I got the feeling that this time it would be different and more intense than the last. I wanted Lola but not necessarily in a sexual way. Maybe I was looking for something more from her, tired of the emptiness of jumping from bed to bed, from partner to partner. I had been disappointed in my recently romances and was searching for something new, something fulfilling. I wondered if I would find it in Lola. We always had a strong connection. Maybe that was a good place to start.

Although Lola and I didn't spend much time face-to-face, each encounter was an incredibly intense experience. Every time we brushed hands, it was electric. Playing with Lola's fingers, we touched each other carefully, hesitantly. I felt like a teenager, like a young virgin boy, experimenting with sex. At times, I wanted to take her anywhere and everywhere but other times, I was shy to express myself. I fantasized about kissing Lola and making out with Lola on her desk. I was on top of her, then beneath her. Then we were lying naked together on the floor.

I couldn't concentrate on my work when Lola was in the same room. The chemistry between us was strong and so was my desire. I had to fight to control myself. Instead, Lola was controlling me. My body throbbed and dampened whenever she was near. I was afraid my hyper-sexuality would drive me to weird situations that would mess up my life even further. I felt out of balance because of Lola and it was about a time to get back to a normal, stable life. But how? I hoped that taking this trip to Alaska was one way to accomplish it.

After the plane landed in Vancouver, Durga and I boarded the cruise ship, which headed all the way up through Glacier Bay. Along the way, we stopped at Ketchikan, Juneau and Skagway, ending up near Anchorage. Durga and I seemed to be the youngest ones on the ship. The other passengers were in their 60s and 70s. They could have been our grandparents. This was great for me, I figured, because there would be no sexual distractions on this peaceful voyage.

The view from my stateroom of the Alaskan glaciers was breathtaking. I had never seen a place as huge and wild as Alaska. I felt very small compared to the towering glaciers, very insignificant. Nature astonished me here and I was kept busy. When we were in port, Durga and I explored our surroundings by hiking, kayaking and biking. It helped me forget about New York and all the troubles I left behind.

Durga and I spoke a lot, about everything—social and political issues as well as personal ones. I was glad to take a little break from my erotic mess of a life. But Durga knew me well and she could tell that something was troubling me. Soon came a difficult and bittersweet discussion that I was trying to avoid: my love and life issues. Out of the blue, Durga asked me, "So, Maggie, how is everything in your heart? Is there someone new?"

Surrounded by mountains and glaciers, I felt small and unimportant. Like my little problems were nothing compared with all of this grandeur around me. After a pause, I told Durga, "Yes…I mean no. She's been in my life for a while, but I think I want something more from her."

Familiar with my personal history, Durga wondered gently, "Are you sure? Or it is just a fascination that won't last long?" Very kindly, Durga tried to help me visualize the truth about myself. Deep down, I knew she was right, but for now, I loved the feeling I had—the newness of love. Or was it lust?

For a moment, I was back in New York. I could see Lola's curvaceous body, her beautiful eyes and smiling face. I enjoyed the beautiful sexual agony of wanting something I couldn't have. My cell phone picture of Lola kept popping up in my mind, silently saying, 'Hello, there,' which is how she answered the telephone when she knew it was me.

Now Lola was everywhere. Damn, I even knew her orgasms. She described them so well in her erotic stories. I felt like I knew every inch of her body, but not really. I felt like touching her, but not yet. My desire was a poison, slowly killing me half a world away from Lola in the wilds of Alaska. I couldn't have Lola. Or could I? It didn't make any sense at all. She was something else, somewhere else. Unreachable. And it was driving me crazy. My sexuality was out of control. I had to change or I would lose my mind.

There I was in this beautiful wilderness but I was not there fully. I wasn't present. I was living in the recent past, dreaming of what might be, wasting my time in another sexual game. Story of my life.

Chapter 13
Meditation Vacation

A few months passed since my Alaska trip without much changing. New York was cold again and getting ready for winter. Chilly winds pulled the autumn leaves from the trees and the streets were covered with a carpet of gold. Before long, the fall would shift into winter and the dry leaves would be exchanged for snow. I tried to savor the last warm days, walking through the streets and Prospect Park, appreciating every last minute of this beautiful season.

Circling the city alone, I felt like the changes in the air reflected the changes within myself. I was tired of the heat and steam of the summer. My life itself was steamy and I needed to cool it down. The long, hot summer seemed to pass by so quickly, with so many huge, exhausting changes within such a short period of time. Sometimes I got the feeling there was a fire in my stomach that burned me from the inside out. I figured it was probably stress but I needed to quench it, literally and figuratively.

I took off my jacket, hoping the cold; strong breeze would help quell the heat within. It did, but too quickly. I found myself freezing and shaking, with my teeth chattering. I buttoned my coat back up to protect myself against the October wind. My thoughts were as heavy as the cloud-filled sky. I just kept walking. I didn't know my destination but it didn't matter. I knew that the way I'd chosen would lead me somewhere, anywhere. I was going nowhere fast anyway. What did it matter? I was wasting my time and energy, and for what? A high-speed, intense New York life? It might be fun but it was empty.

Suddenly everything stopped making sense to me. The world became gray and I was tired of the city and its people. The same city that had appeared vibrant, full of motivating energy and creative people now seemed exhausting and filled negativity. My chosen city was not mine anymore. I'd lost myself in this crowd—my morals, respect for my body and for myself. I became a whore, selfish and emotionless. Where the hell had I disappeared? Where was Maggie in all of this?

Walking aimlessly up and down the streets, I was looking for something but what? I was pretty sure the change needed to start from within. I needed to transform myself if I wanted to transform my life. My trip to Alaska reinforced my love of nature, which I missed so much. Even the green hills of Prospect Park didn't seem like they were enough anymore. I wanted to feel a connection to the natural world again.

Born and raised in the mountains of south Poland, surrounded by wildlife, I missed the hills, lakes and woods. Living in the city, you can't even see the stars in the night sky—the bright city lights mask them. The night sky itself seems to be a big, dark wall, creating distance between you and the universe. I missed the connection with Mother Nature, which, I realized then on that cold Brooklyn street, was a connection with myself. I decided to change my surroundings as soon as I could. But first...coffee.

My brain was melting. There were too many thoughts bouncing through my head. I'd been walking for hours. The wind and cold had exhausted my body and I needed refueling. Looking for a warm place to rest and gather my thoughts, I grabbed a cup of Starbucks, downed half of it, then dashed into a nearby Barnes & Noble bookstore, the perfect spot for temporary, cozy shelter. Without gloves, my hands were frozen and I juggled the coffee cup. Freezing, I couldn't open the door. Not only were my hands numb but the wind pushed the door back every time I tried to open it. When I finally managed to wrestle the door open, I got treated to a nice blast of heat. But the wind slammed the door in my face, leaving me outside in the cold again. It was as though the doors were playing tricks on me, saying, 'Maggie, you want to get in but you're not there yet. You have to fight to get what you need.'

The warmth teased me, tempted me but was just beyond my reach. It was like that for me in life—I had happiness, pleasure, right in front of me, but it always disappeared in a cold blast of air. I gave the door a few more tries until I was finally able to open it and go inside. My battle with the door—and a fear of being left out in the cold—filled me with a strange sort of panic. Although I'd fought so hard to get inside, I suddenly didn't want to be there anymore. The world was such a frigid, unfriendly place. I ached to be somewhere else. There was always a door to be opened, I told myself. There was always a struggle. We constantly entered into different worlds, I thought. Maybe this stupid, stubborn bookstore door was a symbol of my life, a sign of the changes that were to come.

Standing inside the Barnes & Noble, waiting for the wave of heat to envelope my body, I flipped through a handful of books. I found myself in the "Yoga and Meditation" section. I scanned the shelves, searching a book that really spoke to me. Yoga for Dummies and Buddhism for Dummies really jumped out at me. Definitely feeling dumb, I decided to go for them. They looked like a perfect match because that's exactly how I felt at that moment—like a dummy.

Accepting my new label, I flipped through one book. It really caught my interest and seemed like the best guideline for beginners. Little snippets of wisdom jumped out at me. I felt positive, as though it was really possible for me to change. I knew I was in the right place, that it was the right time to begin my transformation. A warmth ran through my body and even deeper than that—into my soul. I felt like these books were talking to me. In response to my dumb questions were so many smart answers.

One quote in particular jumped out at me:

"If you're not working on yourself you're not working at all."

I wrote it down, anxious for a new beginning. I also scribbled down other inspirational sayings and rushed back home to clip them to the bulletin board I kept on my kitchen wall. This way, I would see them first thing in the morning, while having my coffee. Reading them would become an important ritual.

When I woke up the next day and my friend Abel was in my bed. An Arabic guy who'd moved in a couple weeks ago, Abel and I were bunking together for a couple of nights since another friend was visiting New York and had Abel's usual spot on the sofa. It wasn't bad, squeezed together on my little bed with this handsome fellow. Abel was a quiet sleeper, no tossing and turning, because I totally forgot he was next to me at first. People, including my husband, thought there was something between Abel and me. They couldn't grasp that our relationship was just a deep, pure brand of friendship. Sometimes I couldn't believe it either but it was good for me to have a loving relationship that was pure love, and nothing else.

I opened my eyes to see Abel beside me. With a big smile, I snuggled closer and kissed his forehead. He asked, "And what's that for?"

I answered, "For nothing." Then decided to add, "I finally learned to stop kissing friends."

Yes, my fooling-around days seemed to be over. It wasn't just with Abel. When I closed my eyes, I could see myself in the same bed, my bed, with other Platonic friends, the same friends from the trip to New England. The time we spent together in Maine, nothing really happened besides some erotic naïve games. Yet other times, we played fully, consummating our lust to the very end.

Another incident, after a jazz concert in Harlem, my Sugar Mama Mary and I were there with two guys who had been on that Florida tour with us. Tipsy, we took a cab back to my apartment. Sex and alcohol are an aphrodisiac. The four of us started kissing and playing with each other's hands. One of the fellows was around my age and the other had just turned 21 a few days before. Diverse in age but united in lust, we all headed to my bed. Joking around, we really tried to get it going sexually. We kept making silly comments about our bodies, which totally took us off track. But eventually, we ended up having sex. Even though it was a lot of fun, I still had the feeling it was wrong. I'd had too many people in my bed recently and something had to be done to change it. This is why I was especially proud that Abel and I could snuggle, and not have it go any further.

With a smile, I left Abel behind in bed and went to the kitchen to make my morning coffee. I felt different that day, as if there was new something in the air. Not only could feel it but I also felt the changes it could bring. Still half asleep, I bumped into the sofa where my friend Tati, was still sleeping, totally naked. Her lovely, full breasts were shining like two headlights in the dark. This definitely woke me up all the way. Tati must have arrived late last night, after one of her thousands of dates.

Boob-blinded and wide awake by now, even without coffee, I made my way to the kitchen table. I pressed the coffee maker's "on" button and sat down to go over my emails, texts and check on Facebook page. This was my usual morning routine. One message grabbed my attention. It was from Gina, a girl I'd recently met. Gina wasn't my type at all and from the very beginning, I made it clear that I wasn't interested in her. Especially when she informed me how good she was in bed and that she'd already slept with 300 people, more or less. That was too much for even me to deal with. More or less.

I turned off my cell phone and shouted, "No, I'm so not like her...Leave me alone." But why did Gina upset me so much? Had she struck a nerve? Maybe I hadn't fucked 300 people but I definitely slept around without much thought to the consequences. Sex had become an empty bodily function to me, like using the toilet. I did it so much, and without thinking. It was just something my body did.

I turned around and noticed the scrap of paper I'd put on my bulletin board the night before, which said:

> "The secret of health for both mind and body is not to mourn the past, worry about the future, or anticipate troubles, but to live the present moment wisely and earnestly."

Next to it, there was another note which I'd clipped there a few months before. It was a flyer with the headline:

"Meditation and Yoga Retreat in the Catskills"

The flyer had been hanging there for a few months. I'd picked it up at one of the free yoga classes I took in Prospect Park with Beatrice. It was an incredible experience, practicing yoga beneath a stand of tall oak and pine trees with dozens of other people, surrounded by birds, hawks and squirrels, in the lap of nature.

I thought back to the nice, sunny Sunday morning in July when Beatrice and I decided to take a bike ride to Prospect Park. She'd known about the yoga class so we had our yoga mats strapped to our bikes. The trees, hills and people around in Prospect Park always made me feel happy and alive. Some were out walking and jogging while others were already barbecuing. Whole families and groups of friends were picnicking and playing games. I loved being there among all of this good energy. Prospect Park was like Brooklyn's backyard and everyone from all around gathered there.

Beatrice and I spent a lot of time exploring Brooklyn, working on getting in shape and fit for the summer. It wasn't even 10 am and there were already a bunch of people in the Park. We noticed the yoga mats set out beneath the trees and knew we were in the right place. People were either stretching or just relaxing. I found a good spot in the second row, rolled out my yoga mat and began to stretch, trying to relax as well. I tried to forget everything else and concentrated on being fully present in the moment. Indeed, I was 100 percent there, loving the feel of the summer breeze on my skin, enveloped by the sounds of the park around me, of life.

When I opened my eyes, the yoga instructor was standing at the front of the class. I later learned that her name was Evalena and that she and her partner had a yoga studio a few blocks away, called Yoga Sole. Evalena's nicely muscled body, her soothing voice, calm vibe and pretty face immediately made me feel peaceful. I liked her right away and felt her kindness, her beautiful spirit. Who else but a good soul would give a free yoga class to a bunch of strangers in a neighborhood park?

I was able to focus on my yoga practice like never before. It was a combination of being surrounded by nature and being led through postures by Evalena. The energy of my fellow yogis practicing beside me also contributed to my feeling of contentedness. I felt like there was no better place for me to be at moment. All that counted was the here and now.

Evalena stood barefoot on the grass, addressing the class. "Relax," she said, in her lovely, melodic voice, "And let your thoughts be. Whatever you think now is right." This mantra defined my first yoga class in Prospect Park. Evalena's soothing words became my intention and continues to inspire me.

A few days later, I showed up at Yoga Sole. Evalena and I chatted a bit. I decided to take a class there. To my surprise and delight, there were several lesbians in the class, perhaps attracted to Evalena's beauty, pleasant demeanor and hands-on teaching style. I loved the way Evalena's sure, steady hand lingered on her students' backs or shoulders, gently correcting their postures, transferring her wonderful energy to us with a simple touch.

After class, Evalena and I talked about my yoga experience and how I found a sense of peace in this place. I hadn't done much yoga in the past and was eager to learn more. She mentioned a three-day yoga/meditation retreat to a Japanese zendo in the Catskill Mountains which many people in the studio were going to attend and gave me a flyer, which I scanned briefly before going home.

What led me to Yoga Sole? Was I there because I wanted to take a yoga class or because I was so taken with its owner and her calm, quiet beauty? I was injected with an odd sort of energy after my encounter with Evalena. It took me a while to calm down and realize that my attraction was to her positive energy.

To settle down, I took a deep breath and start chanting "Nam-myoho-renge-kyo." It was my daily chant which I used often. For me, it broke down barriers and helped me stay positive. It also helped me realize that I should never give up. I knew I needed to change my attitude toward the outside world and the way I related to others. I longed to know someone else fully and deeply, not merely as a sex object, as a path to my pleasure. Was this even possible?

I put the yoga retreat flyer on my kitchen bulletin board, where it stayed until I noticed it that fateful morning. It's as though it said to me, 'Now is the time, Maggie. Read me again.' I did, paying close attention to details this time. I studied the piece of paper and thought to myself that maybe I should go and try to live with monks in a monastery for few days instead of running away again. Maybe this was something I should try: to stop, think, meditate and change. I knew I would never grow if I didn't do things differently, if I didn't fix the things I was doing wrong. I kept repeating the same mistakes constantly instead of learning from them and moving on. I needed to try something new and at the same time, search deeper within. I needed not only to find my higher self, but to perfect it.

I noticed that the yoga retreat was in a few days. I made a quick call to Evalena. Luckily, there were still a few spots left on the retreat. I reserved a space for me and Beatrice. Besides the possibility of "finding myself," the thought of spending a few days with the great-looking yoga teacher made me smile. I loved her energy and the idea of sharing the same space with her.

On a beautiful fall Friday, I packed my bag, left work early and headed upstate to Livingston Manor with Beatrice beside me. It was one of those beautiful autumn weekends. Although late in the season, the weather was still warm. Even the drive up was gorgeous. The zendo was a simple brown structure in the middle of a magical forest. The colorful red, orange and gold leaves made a brilliant carpet beneath my feet. The zendo faced a tranquil lake, and resembled an impressionistic painting, but one that invited us to take a walk around its beautiful lake. The silence and tranquility of the place reminded me of my Alaskan trip, where I'd felt so connected nature. This time, I wasn't distracted by dirty thoughts about Lola. This time, it was all about looking within myself.

Even though we knew we might be late for the yoga class scheduled for that afternoon, Beatrice and I took a nice walk around the lake. In a sense, we became lost in time. It was so relaxing for both of us to be out there in the woods with nothing to think about but the sound of the birds and the sound of our own breath. It was a wonderful break from the city.

When Beatrice and I got back to the zendo, we found that it was too late to stop in our rooms. The other yogis had already arrived and settled in. Yoga class was about to start. Red-cheeked and overheated from our walk, Beatrice and I managed to find space for our yoga mats in the crowded room. I probably looked like a sweaty mess but it was too late to make a good impression on Evalena. I was so charmed by her appearance and her energy that I missed the whole point of being present in the moment. I so wanted to be noticed by her—but not because I looked and smelled bad. How childish I was.

Many yoga instructors shine with an inner light but none like Evalena. Back then, I didn't understand her beautiful karma fully, probably because I still saw the world as being so sexually-infused that I was blind to most things spiritual. But I was still touched by Evalena's magnetic personality and her stunning aura. I'm glad I was evolved enough emotionally to recognize this because it helped me reach a higher level of consciousness.

Evalena wasn't the only person on the retreat who made a great impression on me. We were all like-minded people there, all sharing the common goal of self-discovery and growth. In the zendo, we all looked the same and wore long, dark, monk's robes when we weren't practicing yoga. We learned traditional Zen meditation, as well as how to eat our meals in complete silence.

The silent meditation at the zendo took a bit getting used to. I never realized how difficult it could be to sit for 40 minutes without talking, without moving. We walked barefoot into the zendo, hands folded and had to sit completely still on a pillow on the floor. It sounds easy until you try to do it! You wouldn't think how twitchy you become during zazen (seated meditation), how little itches start bothering you and how your knees and hips start to ache sitting still for so long. It was also hard not to fall asleep in that cool, darkened room. We all looked like seated Buddha statues.

After zazen, we ate our meal in complete silence, sitting or kneeling at long, low wooden tables. We couldn't start serving or eating until the head abbot began. She was an older woman with a shaved head but a beneficent face. The Abbott reminded me of the Mother Superior at Catholic school. She began passing the large bowls of vegetarian food down the long table. We each put a little of everything into our bowls. Beforehand, we were instructed that we could take all we wanted but that we were expected to eat all we took. We were also taught how to wash out our bowls with tea after our meals and how to wipe them out and store them properly.

The food was surprisingly good, very flavorful. With all of the new things I was experiencing, I was aching to talk to the yogis around me, but talk was forbidden. The only sounds were of our chopsticks hitting our bowls and of our slow, thoughtful chewing. This was very different for me but I was resigned to go through with it, to do what was expected of me.

After our silent meal, we were finally permitted to talk. I tried to break out of my comfort zone and say "hello" to some of the beautiful people at the zendo. They might be strangers now but I had the feeling I would get to know them a lot better by the end of the weekend.

All around me, my fellow yogis were engaged in spiritual conversations. But I couldn't bring myself to join in—I felt too shy. I couldn't even speak to Evalena. I was perplexed about my bashfulness because normally, I dove right into chats and was even a little bit impulsive…as you can see from my past behavior, especially in bars. But I told myself that my trepidation was all right. It was all part of looking within. I decided to spend the rest of my time at the zendo in quiet contemplation for as long as I needed.

During my three day stay there, we practiced yoga and meditated several times each day. Meditating helped me finally understand one thing:

It was me who kept sending sexual energy out into the world. I was the one who was attracting the weird things that happened to me. I was desperately looking for attention...some attention, any attention, even inappropriate attention. I was the one who stimulated every single situation that had happened. It was me who was the predator, not the victim.

In my quietude, I remembered the wise words of Sharon Gannon, a world-renowned yogi:

> "Everything depends on our relationship with others. How we treat others will determine how others treat us. How others treat us will determine how we see ourselves, and how we see ourselves will determine who we are."

It sounds so simple, doesn't it? But as I soon found out, it's very difficult to change. Slowly, I began to understand the cause and effect of my past actions. I understood how this affected my present situation. Who we are is determined by how we treat others. It's our dualistic relationship with the world that we exist in, which we are an inseparable part of, which makes us who we are.

I had gone on this yoga retreat for the wrong reasons—because I had a mini crush on the yoga instructor. I should have gone there only for myself, for inner growth, for change. I should have gone there with the intention of deepening my spiritual practice and getting to know myself better. But it wasn't too late to accomplish this. I vowed to use the time to learn how to meditate and how to listen my inner voice. I would finally master how to control my "Monkey Mind." That's what I called the way my mind worked, jumping from one thing to another, fixated on sex like a horny monkey, jumping from tree branch to tree branch, from partner to partner. I thought I could do it. I hoped I could do it because the way I was living now was destroying me, bit by tiny bit. There was still time to save myself, even though I came to this realization on the last day of the yoga retreat at the zendo upstate.

In an odd way, I think Evalena appeared in my life at the perfect time. It was serendipity. I was finally ready to recognize—and reconcile—all of my past transgressions. Finding Evalena and Yoga Sole, going on that life-changing retreat, helped me realize all of this. To find our true selves, we must learn to calm our inner battles.

"Quiet your mind," Evalena often told us as we began a yoga practice. She inspired me and helped me find the right way to find myself. I also discovered that attraction doesn't necessarily have to be sexual. We can be attracted to people for the positive qualities they have—like calmness, kindness and goodness—not because they might make a good bedmate. This was my moment of awakening, and I promised myself that I would continue the inner growth that I had begun in the zendo's peaceful mountains.

Chapter 14
Big Changes in Little Brooklyn

Flash forward to December 24, 2013. Once again, I'm in the gynecologist's office. This time, she is much nicer to me. It's my birthday, a year after my first visit to her. Somehow, I survived my crazy "Christ Year" and am in her office, getting my annual checkup. This time, the doctor became my best friend. We talked about our lives and she even showed me some family pictures. I felt like we connected, laughing over life.

I told the doctor about my health concerns. I seemed to have my period constantly. She listened carefully then told me that the reason was probably too much exercise and stress. "You need to change your lifestyle, Maggie," she said. "Your body is out of balance."

I was horrified when she told me that she needed to perform cryosurgery on me again. So that was the technical name for what she'd done to me a year ago to this very day. She patiently explained that cryosurgery was the only way to kill the pre-cancerous cells caused by HPV. Cryosurgery freezed off the bad tissue so the cervix could heal and regenerate.

I cringed when I thought of her **stabbing me again with that long spear inserted slowly but sharply into the most vulnerable part of me.** Suddenly, the Good Doctor wasn't my best friend anymore.

For some reason, this time the pain was much more intense than it was a year ago. I felt like it was tearing me apart. The instrument that freezes the cervix was so cold that it felt hot, like she was burning me from the inside out. I bit my lip and renounced all of my sins. Finally, I couldn't take it any longer. I screamed loud, "Please, stop! I promise I'll change!"

In response, the doctor told me, "The HPV has been cured."

Although I was relieved, my first thought was, 'Now I can misbehave again.' But it's too late—I'm already in the process of changing, of bettering myself. However, just having this thought told me that I haven't changed yet and that I still had a long way to go.

There were too many things for me to process. I knew I should change and that I was almost there. But not quite. At my friend Gia's home one evening, she told me, "Maggie I'm talking to you! Are you with us or are you with your girls and boys, texting them?"

"No, not at all," I told her. "There are no more girls, no more boys."

Gia was in shock. "Wow, Maggie. Are you okay? There really must be something wrong in your life. Do you need help?"

I told Gia, "No, thank you. I'm okay. I'm finally okay!"

And the best part was that I was finally starting to believe it myself. I was all right.

Still aching after my cryosurgery, I drove home, staring straight ahead at the road. I was deep in thought, analyzing the wisdom of my choices recently. I don't know what future held but I did know that I learned something in my Christ Year. I lost a few friends, that's for sure. Although I had many happy memories of Rita and Jenny, both Argentineans had disappeared from my life for good. The same thing happened with my Chinese and Turkish girls. I would probably never see Jasmine or Hamsa again. The others I kissed and played with were gone too. They were somewhere in the New York crowd, having fun with someone else, leaving me with nice memories, and still alive after my battle with HPV.

My Sugar Mama Mary was now one of best friends, thank God. Mary was always there for me. So were Beatrice and Gia. Even Arron, my ex, was like family to me. Together almost eight years, Arron and I are still close. And my sweet husband Apollo, I still loved him dearly. He was still such a big part of my life, a good friend. I just couldn't hurt him anymore, though. I know it hurt him when I went out with other girls but I'd come to the realization that I wasn't straight, not even bi. I was a lesbian. I think I needed to force Apollo to leave me, or else he'd never go, and I'd just keep hurting him unintentionally.

And as for me, I was ready to change. Sometimes you need to go through the fire to find the healing that comes afterwards. Sometimes you have to go through hell to get to heaven. I was about to take a huge, important step in my self-discovery process.

Chapter 15
The Best Decision I Ever Made

But first, more hell. For the rest of 2013 and most of 2014, I wandered about aimlessly. I took a trip back to Poland. I went to Israel. Nothing seemed to satisfy me. I always seemed to be searching for something I could never find.

In December of 2014, Beatrice and I had planned a big trip to Thailand, mostly to mediate, but it didn't work out. With no money, I couldn't turn my dream into a reality and decided to postpone it for another time. Not knowing what to do next, I called Beatrice for help. A wine bar called The Castello Plan became the spot for us, our outpost to plan our future moves.

Beatrice was always my voice of reason and I loved her for that. She was blunt and truthful without being hurtful. "Maggie, you just quit your job," she told me at The Castello Plan. "Besides, you just sold almost everything you owned, so there's nothing here for you to stay for. You should leave!"

Although Beatrice was right, I didn't know if I had the heart to leave my beloved Brooklyn. Beatrice was like a bad poker player, putting all of her cards on the table. I didn't know if what she said should make me feel happy or sad. Truthfully, I felt a little bit of both. How could Beatrice, my dear friend, send me off so easily? But I know she only had my best interest at heart, as always. I was at a loss at what to do. I didn't have enough money to go to Thailand and even if I said screw it, and went, I would end up spending what little nest egg I'd saved.

Crying over a glass of Malbec, I doubted everything I ever did, everything I ever knew. Recently, things had gone bad on so many levels. There were too many problems with too many people I knew. Lovers, friends... Friends who were lovers...lovers who were friends. I'd lost so many friends and relationships by getting into conflicts with them. Although I'd ditched the ones who made me unhappy, there was still too much on my plate. I had too much and nothing at the same time. A feeling of emptiness and loneliness was growing inside me. I stepped into the same puddles over and over again, getting soaked to the skin, and not learning to avoid them. Instead of enjoying my life, I was still managing to find trouble wherever I went.

Another thing that was making me miserable was my job. I was tired of teaching because it sapped so much of my energy. I felt that I was constantly on display, like an actor on the stage. At times, it was like my students were stealing my energy, as if they were little vampires sucking out my blood and leaving me half dead. In addition, I had an inner conflict between being an example for my students and behaving just the opposite in my private life. In teaching, as with being a tour guide, people always saw the positive, calm Maggie who respects others and delivers the best service wherever she goes. I was known to say, "Remember, we're always the representatives of our workplace, whatever we do, wherever we go." What bullshit! I was to be discovered and outer later, though.

In the wine bar, Beatrice tapped my hand and softly said, "Don't worry. We'll figure something out, just like we always do. Please believe in the universe. There's a reason things are going this way in your life."

I just laughed out loud. "Where the fuck is this universe and how can I understand what it wants from me?" I asked her. I didn't believe a word of what Beatrice said. I didn't share her "glass half full" outlook on life. I gazed down at my "half empty glass" of wine and broke into tears.

Beatrice kissed my forehead gently, then shocked me by shouting so loudly that all the people in The Castello Plan stared at us openmouthed. "I have a great idea!" Beatrice yelled, barely containing her excitement. "We're sending you to the Bahamas!"

Beatrice managed to calm down enough to tell me about a yoga center called the Sivinanda Ashram Yoga Retreat in Nassau. They had a special arrangement where you stay free for three months in exchange for working there. It sounded like a perfect arrangement: yoga, room and board and work. Three months should be enough time for me to think, plan my future and get my life together. I loved cooking and had experience doing it, so helping out in the Ashram's kitchen sounded great.

My friend went on and on about something called "karma yoga." I stopped Beatrice. "What the hell is karma yoga?" I asked.

"It's a way to help people who feel lost find themselves again," she explained. Beatrice was planning the path of my life like a New Age Kalashnikov. You know, the Russian general, military engineer and inventor—of the AK-47 assault rifle. But Beatrice was using her powers for good.

I shot a series of questions at Beatrice and she answered them all:

"What's an Ashram?"
"What's a yoga retreat?"
"How is it different than the zendo?"

It all centered around self discovery and self awareness, Beatrice told me. That's all I needed to know. I wondered if I was going to stand on my head all day long to get some fresh blood flowing through my head to accomplish this. Could I follow an idea from start to finish about how to live my life thoughtfully and responsibly? Maybe it would take sitting in the Buddha cross-legged position endlessly until I decided to change my life. Would I have to become one of those bald-headed monks living in a Himalayan cave to reach enlightenment?

Like an overnight FedEx package, I was sent to the Bahamas the very next day. But unlike that package, I was full of doubt and fear.

Chapter 16
Paradise

I cut my finger again on the huge, sharp chef's knife. It had already been my fourth or fifth time around, as my karma would soon teach me. Two months have passed since I first arrived at the Ashram. I've been working in the kitchen nonstop without a day off. This was the job I'd been assigned a couple of months earlier during my three months in the Karma Yoga program at the Sivinanda Ashram Yoga Retreat in the Bahamas. I didn't realize what intense physical and mental work it would be.

When I arrived, I was greeted by a paper which I had to read and sign. It said that I was obligated to work six hours a day (which turned out to be seven or more), to do meditation and satsang (which literally means being in the company of "the truth" by sitting with a guru and a group of spiritual students) twice a day and to practice yoga once daily. At the time, I didn't really know what satsang was. It sounded like a kind of Tai Chi or a far-out Eastern practice. And truthfully, I didn't really care what satsang was. If it would further my spiritual evolution, I was all for it.

Not fully understanding I decided to try it and sign the paper. I was there, either way. I had nothing to left to lose anymore. Already, it felt good to smell the sea and hear the sound of the ocean in the distance, to and feel the sun on my face. I sat in a wooden chair beneath a palm tree and read the rest of the literature I was handed. It explained that the day at the Ashram started at 5:30 am and went until 10 pm. Every morning, we meditated for 30 minutes then chanted for 30 more, followed by a lecture about spiritual life that went on until 8 am. Attendance to these morning rituals was a must, as well as for the evening hours, which included 120 minutes of meditation, chanting (this is what "satsang" turned out to be), and another lecture on spirituality.

At 8 am, there was a yoga class that lasted until 10 am, which was a "must" too. After brunch, there was free time but often, this was filled with an interesting workshop led by world-famous spiritualists. Most of the workshops touched upon religion, philosophy, healthy eating and cultural issues. I found them all compelling and didn't want to miss them. At 1:30 in the afternoon, I began my karma yoga, which to me, meant a "non-paying job." It started in the kitchen and ran until 8 pm with no breaks. Later, I learned what "karma yoga" truly mean and also learned the reason for it, but for now, I was in the dark about its significance.

At 8 pm, it was back to my meditation room. Late in the evening, I retreated to my sweet home: a small orange tent that resembled a pumpkin. I had a problem adjusting to it at the beginning of my stay at the Ashram. My air mattress, although big enough, wasn't comfortable. It was nothing like sleeping on my big, fluffy, queen-sized bed back in Brooklyn. The tent itself was only big enough for my mattress. It wasn't tall enough for me to stand in, so to change my clothes, I had to go outside.

The Ashram itself was a peaceful place but the ocean wasn't as tranquil as I had imagined. The loud music coming from the party boats which passed by nonstop on the bay were killing me. I hardly slept, felt exhausted all the time, and due to lack of sleep, was starting to feel depressed. Instead of getting back to shape on Paradise Island, I felt worse than when I had arrived. I was about to give up the first week of my stay there. I felt like my spiritual journey was over, that I'd failed even at being enlightened. I was afraid there was nothing left for me, no one waiting for me back in the cold New York winter. Even Apollo wouldn't be there for me—my husband had finally begun the divorce proceedings I had been urging him to start for months. I didn't know where to go or what to do next. With no money and no hope, I just let it be.

And that was the whole point of me staying at the Ashram, wasn't it? The life lessons I hoped to learn at this magic place. I just needed to adjust, to listen to myself and just let everything go. Finally aware of my past mistakes, I still had to learn how to let go. The old me, Misbehaving Maggie, wasn't helpful either. She was like the little devil you see in cartoons, sitting on someone's shoulder, telling them to do bad things. In my case, my devil was constantly telling me to play sex games and fall for one pretty face or another. I suppose we all have our own demons and this was mine.

My own personal journey began with my spiritual name. There's nothing better than changing your name at the beginning of a transformation. For me, it was something that had significance, something I was striving to become. The day after my birthday, in December 2014, I had a spiritual name initiation. I woke up early in the morning at the Ashram—something I'd already gotten used to—took a shower and cleansed my body I washed away all of the dirt and perspiration to purify myself. Not only did I prepare my body for my naming ceremony but I prepared my mind as well. I cleared it of all negative thoughts. I didn't even speak to anyone as I got ready. I dressed all in white clothing to symbolize my newfound purity. Spotless inside and out and draped in white, I went to receive my spiritual name and mantra inauguration.

I was surprised when Swami B told me, "Ambika is your new name."

"Ambika! Why? I requested Amba!" Irritated that my request was ignored, I hoped it didn't show in my voice.

Very calmly, Swami B informed me, "Ambika is the same person as Amba but the spiritual entity has several names which reflect different aspects of her." He paused and smiled. "Ambika is more cute. It suits you perfectly."

I still wasn't thoroughly convinced. "So, she is still Amba, the Divine Mother?" I wondered.

Swami B nodded. "But not as tough. Ambika has more softness. Isn't that what you're seeking?" he asked calmly, with confidence in his voice. "Softness to balance the harshness of the world?"

"Yes," I admitted. "That's exactly what I need." Then I thought to myself, 'How the hell does he know?' But of course, that's why he's the Swami. He knows you better than you know yourself. Not only do Swamis know where you're coming from but they also know where you are going next.

I still wasn't totally convinced, though. "But I still need to connect with the Divine Mother Nature through her name," I insisted.

"And Ambika is her name," Swami B told me gently. "The Divine Mother Nature but in a different form."

Finally satisfied, I decided to accept my new name and to embrace Ambika. My name would be my tool, my weapon, to destroy my lower, more base existence and exchange it for a higher way of thinking and living.

I'll be the first to admit that I wasn't the best student. I was always late and had to run to meditation to keep my discipline every day. This became my new routine—running and playing "catch up." I tried not to miss meditation, although I sometimes did because I had to stay longer than I'd planned for my karma yoga kitchen job.

Although I enjoyed the act of meditation itself, seated meditation can be a real pain. Literally. Sitting cross-legged for more than 15 minutes is absolutely not a pleasure. For me, it was a torture. After a quarter hour on my square floor cushion, my legs were killing me and my knees became stiff. Soon, I couldn't even feel my legs because they'd fallen asleep. Even stretching them out briefly didn't help. My back also ached in this posture. Maintaining the "V" shape by sitting straight and tall was another challenge to me. My lower back was in agony, especially after working long hours in the kitchen. I couldn't stand straight and kept losing my balance. I waggled to the front and back, as though I was about to topple.

Another challenge in meditation was that my "Monkey Mind" was all over the place—which was everywhere else but quiet. I couldn't silence my inner monkey and was constantly reminiscing about my colorful New York life. In seated meditation, I would picture myself going to bars and having all sorts of wicked fun instead of working hours in the kitchen like the Ashram's Cinderella.

As hard as I tried, my thoughts wandered. 'Shouldn't I focus on the point between my eyebrows and chant my mantra now?' I would ask myself. 'And what happened with the light I should be able to see? Shouldn't I follow it? How the hell can I do this when my head is filled with so many disturbing thoughts?' The more I tried to calm my brain, the more kinky images jumped into my head: Jasmine and me wrestling on the beach, toying with Hamsa's beautiful hands, kissing my co-worker Lola. Instead of fleeing, these thoughts got together for an endless erotic tea party.

Other yogis gave me helpful advice. They told me that when this happened, I should make an imaginary balloon in my mind and send my thoughts away on it. But it was as though my thoughts liked living in my head and refused to get onto that balloon. Besides, I liked those reminiscences too. I felt comfortable to having my old friends and lovers visit. In order to meditate properly, one should be withdrawn from all of their senses and detached. That's what I was taught. Only it wasn't working out too well. How the hell would I ever achieve inner peace if I couldn't learn how to meditate?

Each day, I woke up in my simple, beautiful new home (which was really a tent), and said out loud to myself, "Maggie, you are running away from your old city life. Ambika, you are running to a new, spiritual life." That was my therapy. Something was telling me to keep going and to keep trying to discover the total new me, and make her a reality.

I constantly questioned myself, though. Was it a reality or just a fiction that I created to feel better? So many times I doubted the whole spiritual world, thinking that I couldn't understand it logically so it couldn't be real. Each time my mind doubted, saying, 'This doesn't make any sense,' my intuition ignored it. My intuition was persistent. When my mind played tricks on me, I had to learn how not to act on it, just to observe. In times like this, when I was about to give up, suddenly, out of nowhere, some verse or a word, a dream or a picture of the goddess Durga has appeared in front of me, and convinced me to persevere. Durga became my own spiritual savior because she represented the invincible, something I longed to be. You can say this was just coincidence or else that it was total bullshit. But for me, it was a reality and it helped my spiritual growth. It also helped that I had a good friend with the same name as this unconquerable Hindu goddess.

After it happened thousands of times I started to believe it. More importantly, I was learning how to recognize it. What a wonderful, new experience this was! I became more intuitional rather than intellectual. I finally decided to open my heart to the world and to the universe. I decided to live my life in the present moment, not to worry about the future or over-analyze my past. I wanted to enjoy every single moment of my life in the now. Each day was a fresh one to me from now on. No matter what life brings, good or bad, like Durga the fighter, I decided to break through and approach it with a positive attitude.

My finger was still bleeding from my latest run-in with the kitchen knife. I had to run to the reception area for a Band-Aid and finger condom. Once again. Sunn, a lovely Canadian woman, was at the front desk. Each time I went there with the same problem, Sunn would just laugh. "Ambika, are you back again?" she would tease. Glancing at my bloody finger, she pressed, "Do you want me to give you another condom? A finger condom, I mean. How many have I given you already? Be mindful using it!" she warned, in a flirtatious tone. Or was it just my imagination? Dirty Maggie having her way with me again.

Sunn was always was giving me long, lustful looks that silently told me, "Kiss me." I really tried to resist but I found Sunn extremely attractive. She was a sexy blonde about 40 years old with a nice smile and good sense of humor. Sunn was pint-sized, much shorter than me, but with a high level of energy, especially in this uber-calm Ashram life. As hard as I tried, I still was an aggressive, fast-paced New Yorker. I had a tough time keeping my sexual energy in check too. Sunn's and my sensual repartee, full of double entendres, wasn't proper for this spiritual place where we both worked. But I loved it.

Every time I went to the reception area with a cut finger, Sunn seemed to be there. We started flirting and playing with words. For us, this was as natural as breathing. This went way beyond satvik (which meant "pure" in Sanskrit) ashram minds. We were rajastic and not pure at all. Think of rajastic foods as forbidden fruits—things like coffee, tobacco, alcohol, sweets, heavily spiced and salted items, hot peppers, onions and garlic. It was believed that rajastic foods promoted primitive mentality, aggression, passion and frustration. Oh, yes…and lustful thoughts. Definitely not proper Ashram behavior.

However, the game between me and Sunn was in full swing, and I was thoroughly enjoying it. Especially considering how much I love flirting. One night during meditation, Sunn bent over and softly whispered in my ear, "You have the greatest lips in the whole Ashram. I want to kiss you before you go away."

So, it wasn't just me and it wasn't my imagination. I whispered back, "I'm so game," with no regrets.

Until then, I had been strong and managed to push away any tempting propositions. Before Sunn, there was another girl I really liked at the Ashram. I was getting interested vibes from her as well. I knew Clara and me could have a bit of fun together but I rejected it. I got the feeling that Clara was bi-curious, and I didn't want to become a straight girl's science experiment again. It hurt too much when these women decided that they weren't bi after all.

I also realized that I didn't need these types of games to feel better about myself and feed my ego again and again. At the Ashram, I was learning how to harness my excess sexual energy. I finally felt I was getting a handle on it. I was beginning to understand that confidence doesn't necessarily have to manifest itself through sexual conquests. It comes from something within ourselves, not from others. I just needed to learn how to transform it and use it in a positive way.

I was not only aware of the implications of my actions, but now, for the first time in my life, I was able to say no to the opportunity of becoming involved with Clara. In a strange way, it made me proud to be able to reject her. Believe or not, something deep inside of me shifted and changed. I knew I made the right decision, but there were more temptations to come, one after another. When I was able to resist those advances as well, I realized that I was reconstructing and rebuilding my whole life. This time, it was based on honesty and ahimsa, a word new to me which meant "compassion" or "not to injure." No more silly, selfish decisions to be hurtful to the environment or to myself. I was slowly learning how to "cause no harm" to anyone or anything.

But my decision to be celibate happened before I met Sunn. On that sweet satsang night, her proposition and her childish grin made me laugh. And just like that, I was derailed again. My meditation was over and done with for the night—I could think of nothing but the prospect of kissing Sunn. It brought a smile to my face and a sense of temporary happiness to my soul. I couldn't say "no" anymore. I couldn't refuse the possibility of sharing warm, little kisses and playing sensuous games with her. I liked Sunn a lot. With her, I imagined a simple, uncomplicated dalliance. No judgment, no obligation, just pure pleasure

Sunn and I were beyond being strangers. We'd practiced mediation together, shared meals together, and did yoga together. We were intimate spiritually without having been intimate physically. I had already been at the Ashram for two months, which doesn't sound like a long time, but it was long enough to me to learn how to listen to my inner voice and to keep my emotions in check. But did I want to do this with Sunn?

My goal at the Ashram was to learn how to control my emotions rather than have them control me. I switched off my past and left everything behind. I abandoned New York for the Bahamas in order to transform. I had a job to do, and that was to silence my Monkey Mind which led me to be impulsive, just like a creature in a jungle, moving from tree to tree, from fruit to fruit, without much thought. Thankfully, I'd realized that my Monkey Mind was driving me crazy. I wasn't in charge of my thoughts or my actions anymore when Monkey Maggie took over. The fire deep inside of me was dancing out of control. I couldn't stay still for long without thoughts constantly running my head. Meditation was so difficult because my mind was constantly on the run. Then there were my mostly dirty thoughts to deal with. I really had to work on quieting my mind—and my libido. I almost was there. Almost, but not quite.

I learned the valuable lesson—that yoga shifts us to a completely different level of consciousness. By observing, practicing nonattachment and gathering information from your body and emotions, you are brought back to the heart. The heart then becomes your safe place, your home. Not sex. Not alcohol. Not drugs. The heart. Your heart. This was something that I not only read in one of the yogi's books but that I experienced myself on a deep, deep level.

I loved the new image of myself meditating and doing yoga now. I was smiling more and I was more peaceful since I first arrived at the Ashram. Although I liked the serenity that came with this sense of calm, sometimes I also missed the old, bad Maggie. She was still there somewhere, hiding underneath my skin, sleeping and waiting to be awakened again. This was the inner battle that I had to overcome.

There's so much going on in New York City. It's such a kinetic place. It's always moving, always changing. There's always something to stimulate your senses, only to be replaced by something else the very next moment. New York taught me how to be everywhere at the same time and how to multitask but it didn't teach me how to focus on one thing. New York taught me how to live my life at high-speed and take the energy from the outside world but it didn't teach me how to preserve the sense of stillness that comes from within. New York showed me how to be arrogant and aggressive but it didn't show me how to be good and do good. Although I loved what I experienced and achieved in New York, at the same time, I learned to hate with my whole heart. I became a tough, ignorant human being. The city definitely shaped my personality. I grew stronger in some ways but weaker in more important ones. Although I was taking from the city, its energy burned me out like a spent light bulb.

But it wasn't just me. It was everyone. Living in this hectic city environment, we lose the ability to listen to our own gut, to our own instincts. We ignore the intuition each one of us was born with. We don't follow our inner voice when making decisions. We choose things for all the wrong reasons. Maybe they feel good. Maybe they look good. But we ignore the fact that they might be bad for us. Life decisions shouldn't be based on societal expectations or anyone else's expectations. Instead, they should come from our hearts, and we should listen to our hearts, carefully. But how do you accomplish this in a place of constant noise? Here at the great concert that is New York City, I'm detached from nature. I can't hear its music, its poetry. I can't be one with myself when surrounded by skyscrapers.

To be part of society, we're constantly running: for goods, for a career, for money. But will any of it bring us happiness or fulfillment? No. It's just temporary contentment. It's meaningless. We repetitively try to feed our ego with things, titles and names. It's all about "I, me and mine." Somewhere along the way, we became lost and forgot the true role of humanity and our place in the world: to do good, to be good, to make a positive change, to be that change.

I finally grew to understand what truly living means. I began to feel remorse about the negative things I have done. I decided to fix them and do something positive for the world in return. This became my truth, my karma and goal for now on. The time for change seemed to be crossing my way. I had to find a way to turn Bad Maggie into a positive thing. Just the thought of calling myself "bad" wasn't a conduit to change. I had to stop thinking of myself as bad and putting myself down. I just had to focus on the positive, on the future. Concentrate on Future Maggie, who could—and would—be an amazing human being. I had to turn myself into something useful for the entire planet, not just to get my own needs satisfied. I had escaped city life by running to the Bahamas. Now, instead, I saw that running toward something was my first step in transformation.

Everyone else was more tolerant with me than I was with myself. Prana, my spiritual mentor, who was also the kitchen's head chef, told me as we worked side by side, "Ambika, first of all, be patient. Do not look for the fruits of your action. They will come automatically when you are ready. Don't rush anything just observe." But I became easily frustrated, even when chopping carrots for dinner. "Look," he continued. "You must let it go and be mindful. Just focus on what you are doing now. When cutting carrots think of carrots. When reading a book, think of reading it. When meditating, think of meditating. This is the embodiment of mindfulness."

"Very simple," I told him, hoping the irony wasn't lost with him. Mindfulness...I associated it with using a finger condom because that's what I heard the first time I cut a chunk out of my finger. With sarcasm, I said: "Yes, Chef, I know what mindfulness means very well." I then focused on the huge bag of carrots I had to mindfully chop and meditate while doing so.

Practicing concentration, I focused intently on my carrot-chopping task—and tried not to cut myself again. But when I looked up, there Sunn was, standing in front of me in the kitchen, with a wide smile, just for me. She had probably been watching me for awhile already.

Sunn gave me an intense look, ran her hand through her long, blonde hair and said quietly, "Maggie, you still remember our secret, right?"

In response, I smiled back. "Of course. Whenever you're ready, I'm ready." And with the big, kitchen knife in my hand, I waved it in the air, giving her a sign to keep it quiet and to go away...for now. Sunn just laughed. Ignoring my plea for silence and discretion, she shouted out, "Maggie I love you, love you!"

I loved her too, but not only her. I loved most of the people there at the Ashram. I didn't respond as Sunn strolled away, still laughing.

Our kissing agreement was so pure, with no commitment, no attachments and full of love—but the friendship sort of love we all shared at that magical place. Everything was soaked in love at the Ashram. You almost felt as though you were swimming in an ocean of love. Everyone was so kind, so polite. We were all there for similar reasons—for analyzing and cleaning up our private lives. Besides, we really supported each other on the path of change and spiritual growth. When someone became emotional, we hugged them. That really didn't happen in the outside world unless you knew that person. But at the Ashram, people approached each other with huge smiles. The understanding was built in because we were all traveling down the same road. It was like a different planet. It was a million miles away from the harsh reality of New York, a place full of strangers where people were always trying to get over on each other, cheat each other, take from each other. Both karma yogis and guests lived in the present moment. No past or future existed, which was a wonderful, liberating feeling.

At the Ashram, I learned how to fulfill every moment of my life, finally understanding what mindfulness means. Sometimes we heard crying coming from a tent somewhere beneath the palm trees. But we never intruded—we just let that person cry. We all knew that you needed to empty out everything in order to make room for new, better things to come. It's like having a full glass of water; it has to be empty before it can be full again. It's so simple in theory but difficult to practice. You need to open every single cell of your body and heart in order to let everything go.

Everyone at the Ashram had those intense, emotional moments but there was always someone nearby to hold them in their arms, to let them cry. No one ever encouraged them to stop crying—it was important to let out those pent up feelings. We knew they would finish crying—eventually—but while they sobbed there would be strong arms around them to let them know they were loved. The shelter of someone's arms was only temporary; the shelter of love was everlasting. To be enveloped in an atmosphere full of love and without judgment was so different than what you experienced in the outside world. I promised to take that sentiment with me when I left the Ashram, and to share it with as many people as possible. This is one of the reasons I've written this book—to teach, to share, to help others grow.

With the finger condom reminding me of Sunn's promise, I turned my mind from the humongous bag of carrots and analyzed the thoughts that ran through my head. I was in a totally different headspace than meditation—I was in the Land of Lust. I tried to say "no" to these distracting thoughts, but they didn't want to leave. They seemed to like their new home—inside Dirty Maggie's dirty mind.

Instead of fighting them and chastising myself for having these nasty thoughts, I decided to do nothing but accept them. And that was that. Finally, I had learned how to control my desires—by practicing acceptance.

My goal on this trip to the Ashram was to calm down, find balance and begin focusing on things that were more important than fun and sex. They had totally dragged me down. I had simplified my life and was now connecting with nature in the hope of finding balance, stability like a solid, sure tree with roots firmly planted in the ground. Then, and only then, would I be able to "fix" myself.

"Balance, balance, balance," became my mantra instead of "Sex, fun, and excitement." I was almost there, but then Sunn came along. I asked myself, 'A little love and romance on the Ashram without attachment and pain couldn't hurt, could it?' I knew the answer. Although sex wasn't strictly forbidden here, I knew that it often got in the way of true enlightenment. But then there was the light of Sunn's warm smile, which I wanted to bathe in, especially when she smiled just for me. There was Sunn's gorgeous, long, golden hair, which I imagined felt like silk. Then there was Sunn's...

I stopped myself and moved to another kitchen task. This was my karma for now—peeling vegetables. It was my "present" and I should stick to it for the time being. Enriched with this new knowledge, I decided to wait and observe in matters concerning Sunn. Every morning, before I even got out of bed, I reminded myself, 'Maggie, you control sex, sex doesn't control you." This was my morning mantra, and it was a powerful one. I believed that most of my problems stemmed from sex—from letting it rule me and control my every thought, my every move. At the Ashram, I was taking giant steps toward achieving balance in my life, acknowledging the fact that I couldn't run from one extreme to another, from one bed to another. I was beginning to take responsibility for my actions, thinking of the results and changes they would bring to my life and the lives others before thoughtlessly taking action.

Finally, I had learned that anything I did—anything we all do—creates a reaction. On this planet, we are responsible for others as well. I don't believe our relationships can be emotionless because they always create energy, they create vibrations. What we give out, what we cause, will return in exactly the same way. From now on, I promised myself that I would I focus on yoga and especially on my headstand, which still needed a lot of work.

It's already been two years since I started focusing on my yoga practice. I realized that I couldn't master the headstand while still being angry at the whole world, including myself. I couldn't believe the fear I had about standing on my head! Besides the obvious issues of balance, I had another—the lack of patience. Just as I did in many aspects of my life, I rushed trying to get into a headstand as fast as I could. Even when trying to accomplish a difficult yoga posture, I was chasing myself and missing the whole point of the exercise. It wasn't as much about reaching the goal itself but the journey you take to get there. In headstands and in life, we should savor every moment of learning and be completely in the moment. The future will come no matter what we do, but we alone create the present, the right now. As much as we focus and put effort into the present, there will be side effects, things we have no control over. But what we do have control over is the present, this perfect moment we are living in.

More than two years ago, while cutting potatoes in the Ashram's kitchen, I asked Chef Prana, "Why can't I do a headstand? I thought I had a strong arms and strong abdomen muscles, so why can't I do it? It's just not working for me. What am I doing wrong?"

Prana didn't pause in his chopping when he told me, "Ambika, it's simple. You're just not ready yet." I looked at him incredulously, then he continued, just as calmly, "Keep practicing. Trust yourself and the universe. Don't rush. Just take it step by step. When you get balance in your life, it will transfer to your head and you will do the headstand effortlessly."

Prana saw disbelief in my eyes. "Trust me. Trust yourself," he repeated.

After satsang one evening, Sunn, a few others and myself kissed. It was at the sumptuous Atlantis Resort, which is also on Paradise Island, just like the Ashram. (But it's so very, very different!) We were having a party the night before I was to take my Teacher Training Course. Although the party was great fun, I found myself falling back onto my misbehaving ways, just briefly. Instead about getting upset, I considered it a means to say goodbye to the old Misbehaving Maggie. With the kiss we all shared, Maggie was gone and Ambika was born.

I thoroughly enjoyed the kisses but they were totally unnecessary. I realized that I didn't need my fed ego to grow anymore, to feel attractive, to feel wanted. I finally understood that I was not attached to anything: not the sexual attention I once craved, not to people or my body. It was an awakening, a revelation to me.

Since then, I have decided to treat my body like my temple. Not everyone is permitted entrance to that temple, just a chosen few. I have decided to keep my temple clean with a deep respect for myself. I finally became aware of this and was ready to take the next step. I cleansed my body of alcohol and sex, refusing to have either for another six months to complete my cleansing ritual.

To further my journey, I decided to become an example for others. For me, the best way to accomplish this was to become a yoga instructor. This obligates you to be pure and honest to others, as well as to yourself. Not only did I sign up for a yoga teacher training but I followed through with it and finished it. My friend Beatrice joined me later in the Bahamas and completed her yoga teacher training as well.

I am on a mission from now on to share what I have learned. Today, I realize that it wasn't New York or things or people who were causing my unhappiness and disharmony—it was me. And it's those things, the heartbreak I experienced, the health crisis I went through, the depression, the drunkenness, which brought me to the threshold of awakening where I stand right now.

I'm in the right place. This is the right time. The misguided sexual energy I once had is now harvested and has been transformed into self-realization.

An important step in my growth, in my evolution, was writing this book. I'm not sure what the next step will be or where it will take me. All I know is that I'm ready to follow that path, wherever it will lead.

Namaste.

Epilogue

I am in a beautiful place in my life right now. I am so happy to be here—on the planet, and in New York. I feel that it's just the beginning of my spiritual path, a place where I can deepen my practice.

Two months ago, I visited Peru with my friend, Durga. The trip just confirmed what I learned in the Ashram, and during the last year in general. Touring the land of the Incas, I discovered that their beliefs, ethics and life were based on a deep connection with nature and the universe. Respect for each aspect of nature—including people and animals—is what they value the most. This is what I want to contribute to the world.

With this approach in mind, I still work as a tour guide but now I apply to my job the knowledge of our great purpose and try to show people the uniqueness of New York. It's a place where everyone can live in peace with little judgment. When taking groups down to Washington, DC, I point out figures like Abraham Lincoln and Martin Luther King, the impact they made on history, and especially their beliefs centered around respecting others.

I truly believe the credo, "Think globally, act locally," and try to embody it.

I don't see people as vampires anymore.

I love to cook and revel in staying in the quiet zone so I can strengthen my mindfulness practice.

My Apollo, the second planet in the same orbit, is still with me. He accepts the fact that one day I may leave him for a woman again when I find the right one. But we decided not to project the future, just to exist in the here and now, to live in the moment and see how things go.

To survive, I've cobbled together a few careers which I like, which make me feel fulfilled, which make me feel like I can make a difference. I also travel to home to Poland occasionally to teach yoga. Basically, I earn enough money to satisfy my needs here in New York and to indulge in my world travels when I can afford to. Money, achievements, social status and career are not my goals any more, though. My goals are much deeper than that.

I felt this was a good time in my life to write all of this down, to examine where I've been to help myself stay on the path. It occurred to me that my story might help others as well. I would like to use some of the proceeds from the book's sales (if there are any!), to donate money to those in need. I'd also like to save some for my trip to India, which is coming soon. And guess who's coming with me? None other than Miss Jenny, herself. Now, how did that happen?

Just before my trip to Peru, I received a Facebook message text from Jenny, after two years of silence. I wasn't surprised, though because when I was at the Ashram, I constantly thought of her during meditation. Jenny was the one who introduced me to yoga. Maybe my thoughts during meditation summoned her. But I was happy when she finally contacted me.

Jenny and I find ourselves at important crossroads of our lives again, and it's funny that our lives have once again intersected. She was planning a trip to India to comploto her advanced yoga training and I was too. So, we decided to go together. Karma. But life is funny that way, isn't it?

Malgorzata "Maggie" Ambika Zurowska
December 2015
Brooklyn, New York

Acknowledgements

Special thanks are due to Jonathan Deutsch. I shared my life stories with him, and one day Jonathan just gave me a journal, and said, "It's time you start to write this down."

Thanks also to Christine Zagari LoPorto, always busy, but always eager to read my chapters and offer advice, regardless of where she was—at work, driving home or mopping floors. Her excitement for this project, her interest in the tiniest details and dedication to my pursuits always motivated me to continue to write and to be inspired.

I also would like to thank those who gave me constant support like Kat Janicka, all of my friends especially Iwona Bardecka for always being there for me.

My editor Catherine Gigante-Brown, who took my rough English and helped express my thoughts in an engaging, inclusive way.

And thanks to Justyna Faustyna Milczuk for designing the beautiful cover.

About the Author

Malgorzata "Maggie" Zurowska was born in Poland. In search of adventure, she came to the United States in 2002. Based in Brooklyn, Maggie spends most of her time traveling, her hobby in addition to things culinary. She contributed a chapter on lizard soup to Jonathan Deutsch and Natalya Murakhver's book They Eat That?: A Cultural Encyclopedia of Weird and Exotic Food from around the World.

Made in the USA
Middletown, DE
14 June 2017